DEEP IN THE HEART OF TEXAS

Reflections of

Former Dallas

Cowboy Cheerleaders

St. Martin's Press New York

DEEP IN THE HEART OF TEXAS

★

Suzette, Stephanie and Sheri Scholz

★

Three former Dallas Cowboys Cheerleaders
with John Tullius

Deep In the Heart of Texas: Reflections of Former Dallas Cowboy Cheerleaders.
Copyright © 1991 by Suzette Scholz Derrick, Stephanie Scholz Neurohr, Sheri
Scholz Carpenter. All rights reserved. Printed in the United States of America.
No part of this book may be used or reproduced in any manner whatsoever without
written permission except in the case of brief quotations embodied in critical articles
or reviews. For information, address St. Martin's Press, 175 Fifth Avenue, New
York, N.Y. 10010.

Design by Diane Stevenson SNAP-HAUS GRAPHICS

Library of Congress Cataloging-in-Publication Data

Scholz, Suzette.
       Deep in the heart of Texas : reflections of former Dallas Cowboy
    Cheerleaders / Suzette, Stephanie, and Sheri Scholz.
            p.   cm.
       ISBN 0-312-06334-2
       1. Dallas Cowboys Cheerleaders—Biography.   2. Scholz, Suzette.
    II. Scholz, Sheri.   III. Title.
    GV956.D3S32   1991
    791.6′432′097642812—dc20   91-20417
                                                                       CIP

First Edition: September 1991

10 9 8 7 6 5 4 3 2 1

TO MOTHER
WITH LOVE
FROM SUZETTE, STEPHANIE, AND SHERI

Foreword

STEPHANIE

It's late afternoon in San Diego, and the sky over Mission Bay is outlined by the multicolored sails of the catamarans patrolling the beach. Our newborn daughter is sleeping soundly at my side in the hotel room while I assemble my thoughts and feelings about this book.

The landscape kissed by the California sun makes the grounds look like the Garden of Eden. Everything is green and lush. The only sounds are the distant ocean waves. Even though this trip was intended for rest and relaxation, I cannot forget the months of preparation and toil it has taken to prepare this story for publication.

My briefcase is opened and overflowing with correspondence and notes, and piles of paper surround me. The red message light on the telephone in the middle of the bed has been blinking all morning. I ignore everything for the moment in order to reflect on the past year and a half.

Soon, in my mind, I am back in Texas.

It is February, 1989, and the Dallas Cowboys Organization has just changed ownership for the second time in the team's history. Bum Bright has sold the Dallas Cowboys to Jerry Jones, an Arkansas oil man. Then Jones turns right around and fires legendary head coach, Tom Landry, and replaces him with Jimmy Johnson, coach of the national champion Miami Hurricanes, and, as it turns out, Jones's old college roommate.

★

DEEP IN THE HEART OF TEXAS

Shock waves roll across the nation. Will Dallas ever recover? The economy was in a turmoil, thanks to failed banking schemes, real estate deals gone sour, and the decimated oil and gas industry. Now, to add insult to injury, our beloved Cowboys—"America's Team"—is in shambles. Dallas is devastated.

The memories all come rushing back.

The new regime made sweeping changes in the Dallas Cowboys Organization. Suzanne Mitchell, director of the Dallas Cowboys Cheerleaders, stepped down and Debbie Bond, her assistant for many years, took over the reins. But Bond's tenure as a director was short-lived. She resigned after Jerry Jones reportedly announced dramatic changes to be made in the cheerleading program.

My mother called my sisters, Suzette and Sheri, and me just as the news broke about Jones's tampering with the Cheerleaders' image. "If there has ever been a moment in time for the three of you to write a book, it is now. Each of you has such a different perspective on the organization. The real story of the Dallas Cowboys Cheerleaders has never been told through the eyes of a Cheerleader. Now is your opportunity to tell your side."

We met to discuss Mother's suggestion. The concensus was that it was a worthwhile and exciting project to consider but it seemed an impossibility to accomplish. That evening, Suzette and Sheri slept soundly, but I tossed and turned. Try as I might, I could not get Mother's words out of my mind. I would be on the verge of dozing off and I would hear her say, "Now is your opportunity to tell your side."

After my husband and I took a long weekend road trip to New Orleans, we arrived back in Dallas with an entire notebook full of thoughts and ideas about the book. It was beginning to gel for me as well as my sisters.

Our desire to share this bitter-sweet story of hope and

★

despair took the three of us to New York, where we found a literary agent, Wendy Lipkind, who guided our dream, and a publisher, St. Martin's Press, who shared our vision.

SHERI

After securing a publisher, we began the monumental task of locating more than 150 former Dallas Cowboys Cheerleaders. That required tracking down phone numbers and addresses, and crisscrossing the nation in order to reestablish old relationships and conduct interviews.

Following an extensive research process, we were able to unravel mysteries and recollections of individual Cheerleaders that, when linked together, tell the real story of the Dallas Cowboys Cheerleaders. Everyone interviewed was enthusiastic and willing to give of her time to help us put together the pieces of the puzzle.

I had followed in my sisters' footsteps and become the only third sister in the history of the Cheerleaders to join the squad, but I was unprepared for the challenge of putting together the story of our experiences.

In my dimly lit room now, I complete a thought on my legal pad for a chapter in the book. I flash back to many of the peaks and valleys of being a Dallas Cowboys Cheerleader. Although much of it is painful to relive, I believe my story will help others who, in the course of realizing their dream, have encountered a different reality behind it.

SUZETTE

My hectic day is coming to a close. Final revisions of the manuscript are underway. All update phone calls have been made to the Cheerleaders who were interviewed. It's almost midnight and my family is asleep. The only sound is the soft ticking of the mantle clock.

Only now am I able to concentrate and focus on the piles

★

of scrapbooks, newspaper clippings, and magazine articles scattered on the floor in front of me. This is the final step in bringing the drafted manuscript to life.

Emotion overwhelms me as I sort through printed pieces of my life that spark fond memories. There was that first bitter-cold Christmas I spent with our troops in Korea; our performance at half time in Super Bowl XII; the battle of Cheerleaders versus Cowboys on Family Feud; the thrill of meeting Bob Hope in person; and that once-in-a-lifetime sensation of strutting onto the field in Texas Stadium for the first time as a Dallas Cowboys Cheerleader. It's hard to believe nine years have passed since I wore that uniform.

I continue to leaf through the pages of material until I come across an album of photographs taken at our first and only Dallas Cowboys Cheerleaders Reunion held December 2, 1989, at the home of our former director, Suzanne Mitchell.

It was an evening filled with mixed emotions for everyone, especially Suzanne who had called us together one last time to bid farewell to the "ladies" who had cheered during her 14-year reign. We laughed through reminiscences and shared the joy of seeing old friends and hearing of marriages, births, and job promotions. We consoled those who described how divorce, disappointments, and hardships had resulted in fragile self-esteem.

That night was a turning point for my sisters and me. The reunion confirmed our belief that as a chapter in professional sports was coming to an end, the story of our role in the history of the Dallas Cowboys needed to be told.

This book is more than a compilation of stories about the Dallas Cowboys Cheerleaders. It's our story of growing up in Texas. And it's the story of the Texas mystique—an American Dream still very much alive today.

★

Acknowledgments

This book is a tribute to every Dallas Cowboys Cheerleader that has proudly worn the internationally famous royal blue and white uniform. We are eternally grateful to each girl interviewed, who so graciously gave of her time, providing us with details to reconstruct past events. This book was written based on the trust and friendship of many of our fellow squad members, and would not have been possible without their support.

During our initial struggle to create the book, Michael Levenson opened many doors. He also helped us locate a literary agent, Wendy Lipkind, who has been our guide and the glue that has held our project together.

We want to thank Chris Connor and Mary Candace Evans for their efforts in helping us gather and construct material for our first proposal.

The three of us are extremely grateful to Jim Fitzgerald and St. Martin's Press for believing in us and having the vision to publish our book; and Jim's assistant, Alex Kuczynski, for her invaluable help. A special thanks goes to Suzanne Fitzgerald Wallis, our editor, who breathed her magic into the manuscript and went above and beyond to ensure all details were covered in the book's development and publication; and to her husband, Michael Wallis, for additional material that was needed in the final rewrite of this book.

The front cover was a collaborated effort by Michael Con-

★

nor, our photographer, Lydia Duron and Tressia Bond, our makeup artists, and Tony Fielding and Michael Lathan, our hairstylists. The clothes were designed by Mitzy for Sable.

The back cover was photographed by Bob Mader. Lydia Durón was our makeup artist and Clint Wheat was our hairstylist. The clothes were by Wild West Outfitters and North Beach Leather.

We want to extend our gratitude to Jim Connor for his insightful wisdom and expertise during the entire writing and editing process.

Mother, because of you, it was not by coincidence that we became the only three sisters in the history of the Dallas Cowboys Cheerleaders. You raised us to always believe in ourselves, and your unconditional love and support have helped us over many obstacles in life. You have instilled in us traditional values, morals, and beliefs and taught us, above all, that no mountain is too high to climb. You are the epitome of the Texas woman with your strength, femininity, class, and charm, and we were fortunate to learn from the best.

Mamie, you have always been magical in our lives. Your constant presence provided us with stability and allowed us to dream and explore our wildest fantasies, all in the protective environment of your love. Your sense of humor and beauty are unparalleled, and we feel blessed to have you not only as our grandmother but as our friend.

Daddy, thank you for our wonderful years growing up as a family. It was through your example that we learned about the importance of education. All the tap and ballet classes would not have made a difference in our life if we had not developed our minds as well.

Butch, Hunt, and Bill, words cannot express the love and appreciation we feel toward each of you and our children.

★

You are our foundation, our inspiration, and our source of strength. We want to thank you for always being there for us.

Hunt, from the conception of this work to its completion, your light has led us forward. You were always there to celebrate our victories along the way, and to pick up the pieces when we fell. Through your encouragement and commitment, we have been able to see our book come to life. We thank you.

★

DEEP IN THE HEART OF TEXAS

Daddy got "big rich"—as they say in Texas—at about the same time my sister Suzette and I became Dallas Cowboys Cheerleaders.

Of course, he wasn't alone. Almost overnight, during the late seventies and early eighties, many people in Dallas made a great deal of money. All over town they cruised in luxurious Silver Clouds and Excaliburs. Many bought hundred-foot yachts, christening them with names like "LBO" and "Land Swap," after the deal that financed them.

There was a light-headed feeling around the city. It was as if we'd all stepped out into the hot, blinding sunlight after a four-margarita lunch; as if Fourth of July was everyday and fireworks filled the sky like exploding stars.

We were all caught in that euphoria of sudden money. Everything we touched seemed 24-carat. No one ever imagined that real explosions were coming and that a lot of what we held so dear would soon go up in smoke.

I remember the first regular season game that I cheered for the Cowboys. Suzette was driving the new red "Z" that Daddy had bought for her, floorboarding it down Central Expressway. We were always running late and today was no exception.

It was a hot Sunday morning in August. The streets were still wet from an early morning rain, so when Suzette made a sharp right onto Stemmons, the car spun completely around

★

and ended up facing the way we were headed. We were lucky there were no other cars in sight. Suzette and I just looked at each other for a second and sighed. "You all right, Stephanie?" she asked. When I nodded, she stomped down on the pedal and we were off again. We didn't get very far before one of Dallas's finest spotted us from his white cruiser. He finally caught up with us just before the entrance to the Carpenter Freeway.

From the rear-view mirror I watched the officer get out of his car; he had a deep scowl on his face. It was a lazy Sunday morning and we'd just interrupted his coffee break. I could see his Dunkin Donuts bag up on his dash and a few crumbs still on his cheek. Two girls racing up one of the main drags in Dallas at double the speed limit made for an unhappy trooper.

Suzette reached over into the backseat and grabbed one of our pom-poms and put it between us for the cop to see. This was in case the warm-ups and makeup of these two decked-out blondes didn't give him a clue as to who we were.

"Just what the hell do you ladies think you're . . ." he started to say. But before he could finish, Suzette yelled, "We're late for the game!"

He looked at the pom-pom, then at Suzette, and then over at me. Our royal blue and white silky warm-ups, which fit like the skin on a seal, were recognizable to every self-respecting male in Texas; that is if he still had a pulse. In an instant, he realized we were wearing the uniform of the Dallas Cowboys Cheerleaders.

"Don't worry girls," he said. The officer rushed back to his cruiser, jumped in, turned on the lights and the siren, pulled up beside us, and yelled out the window, "Follow me!" The police car turned onto the Carpenter and we followed right behind. It was exhilarating to fly down the freeway at 90 m.p.h., the 280Z going about as fast as it could. Looming

★

off in the distance was the mammoth blue and silver monolith where the Dallas Cowboys played their games: Texas Stadium.

With no time to spare we screeched up to Gate 6. Suzette pulled up alongside the trooper, jumped out and gave him a big kiss on the cheek, and we were off. There were exactly 93 seconds to get to the locker room before we were late. The tunnel into the stadium was only twenty feet away but it might as well have been 20 miles. Clogging the entrance were photographers and reporters, all madly snapping away, yelling at us to look this way and that.

I looked over at Suzette and screamed, "What are we going to do?" Then Noni came barreling through, clearing the crowd like Moses parting the Red Sea.

Noni was the nice lady who, like an unmuzzled pit bull, guarded the door to the Dallas Cowboys Cheerleaders' dressing room. During the week she was a nurse at St. Paul's, but on Sunday she was the security guard that absolutely no one got past. Noni was as tough as two nose tackles, but to us she was like a mother hen. When she finally reached us, Noni grabbed Suzette and me by the wrists and charged back through the crowd. Suddenly we were in the locker room with plenty of time to spare. Eight seconds.

When I opened the door to the locker room, what hit me most was the smell of hair spray and what seemed to be over twenty brands of perfume. It was a strong, high-pitched scent that went perfectly with the electric excitement building in and around us. From all over the Southwest people had flown in on private jets or arrived in chauffeured limos. There were station wagons filled with waiting families—dad, mom, Billy Bob, and a couple of the neighborhood kids. There were cowboys in pickups with a can of Lone Star in one hand and a rifle racked in the rear window.There were chartered Greyhounds filled with people from all over Texas, and from

★

as far away as Albuquerque, Tulsa, and Texarkana. Every-one was coming to see the biggest, most important event in the whole Southwest, a Dallas Cowboys football game.

When we all arrived kick-off was still two hours away, but there were only about 30 minutes left to get ourselves looking fabulous. The Cheerleaders' locker room was a bare-walled, 10 by 20 foot concrete box with a wooden bench running along one wall and a lone full-length mirror propped up in a corner. As we all sat on the floor, our make-up cases on the bench, curling irons and blow dryers busy at work, we gossiped about our boyfriends.

"Oh, I met the cutest guy, *Laurie!*"

"Where?"

"Cafe Dallas."

"Oh, I bet I know him. What's his name?"

At around 11:30, Suzanne Mitchell, the director of the Cheerleaders, yelled, "Okay, girls. Get in your groups." And for the next hour and thirty minutes we danced. Lined up in a little box of a room that barely held us all, elbow to elbow, shoulder to shoulder, we practiced the routines we'd be doing that day at the game. There was no room for the full kicks, so instead we'd take little bitty steps and make shorter hand movements, all in time with the tape recorded music.

Rehearsing before a game was not that unusual. In fact, I was always rehearsing. In my sleep, or even pushing my basket down the aisle of the Food Pantry, I'd be practicing my dance routines. Dancers do the same thing. In actuality that's what a Dallas Cowboys Cheerleader is—a dancer. Not only a cheerleader.

Being a Dallas Cowboys Cheerleader was like being a member of a Broadway chorus line. Instead of playing before a packed house of 1,500, we danced in front of 65,000 people

★

with 20 to 25 million at home looking on. If I missed a beat or fell flat on my face, a good part of the U.S.A. saw it.

There are quite a few misconceptions about the Dallas Cowboys Cheerleaders and one of them is that we led cheers. Ironically, in the entire three years I was on the team, from 1979 to 1982, I never once led a cheer. The cheerleaders didn't do the usual "Go! Fight! Win!" We'd sometimes yell, "Yaaaaaaaaaa! Go Cowboys!" or flip a few cartwheels after a big play, and we'd generally go nuts after a touchdown, but organized cheers? Never! We were dancers. Most of the Cheerleaders were even trained as such. Our choreographer, Texie Waterman, was a New York-schooled jazz dancer who had performed for years on Broadway. With her talents, our performance at every game looked like a Revue.

As we put the final touches on our makeup and hair, Suzanne quieted us down. "Ladies, you have worked very hard all summer, and each of you has earned the right to wear the uniform this season. It is with honor at this time that I would like to present each rookie with the gold Dallas Cowboys Cheerleaders ring." Goosebumps ran up and down our bodies as we placed the symbol of achievement on our finger.

"Okay girls. Five minutes!" Suzanne yelled. It was showtime. We paraded down the ramp in two lines. When we reached the end of the tunnel my heart stopped. That's when the enormity of the whole thing hits home.

When Suzette and I first arrived that day, there were no fans inside the stadium, but when we came out of the locker room two hours later, it was filled with cheering people. I could see the crowd crammed all the way to the upper reaches of the huge blue and silver bowl. There were banners everywhere—"Beat the Eagles," "We love you Suzette," "Go Cowboys." The Cowboy Band played as the players were moving off the field after warming up. The stadium was all

★

color and noise. My breath was short and my skin was tingling from the excitement.

It's impressive enough just being a fan. But a fan is just a temporary visitor who rents a small space for the day. As a Dallas Cowboys Cheerleader I felt the *whole* stadium was my space and I had a responsibility to the people who filled it.

When I walked into the stadium for that first game I was overwhelmed and frightened, but inspired, too. That's when it finally dawned on me that I was a part of the Dallas Cowboys! I was part of that world famous organization that included legends like Tom Landry and Roger Staubach. I was in the major leagues. The best of the best, not just in Texas but in America.

As the announcer boomed out over the loudspeaker, "And now ladies and gentlemen, the internationally acclaimed Dallas Cowboys Cheerleaders!" I thought my heart was going to explode.

"Okay, Let's go!" Suzanne yelled.

Suzette, who was at the head of the line, turned quickly around, gave me a wink, and then led us out into the stadium across the field like 36 drum majors. Every single fan in the place leapt to their feet and screamed in an earsplitting crescendo that bounced off the back wall and rolled toward us, drowning us in a din of love. It was sometimes hard for us to believe how much the fans all over Texas loved us. But they did. We were their girls, and we represented everything they liked about Texas and the way they were brought up. Whenever they saw us, in the stadium or out, they cheered and screamed and shouted their love.

The performing is what kept bringing us back. Being in front of a sea of people cheering their heads off was a great big high. It was like 65,000 volts of energy rushing through us. It was a charge no drug can possibly match. That's when

★

I knew that every agonizing and grueling moment of practice was worth it.

The intoxicating applause and the clamor wherever we went, however, were not our only motivations. It was the fact that we'd all been brought up to believe in everything that the Dallas Cowboys Cheerleaders stood for—the institution of football and cheerleading. When I pranced out on that field I was fulfilling my childhood dreams. And 65,000 people were screaming their approval, shouting in deafening emphasis that they shared my dreams.

That summer we had record heat waves in Dallas. It was over 105° for eighteen days in a row. The playing field lies at the bottom of a huge bowl where there's never even a little bit of a breeze. That day, temperatures down there soared above 120°! When we walked out into the tunnel and popped our pom-poms at our hips, the sweat already beading on our arms made us feel like we were glasses of ice tea. We dance-ran—step-step-step-ball-change, step-step-step-ball-change—nearly 150 yards down the field as fast as we could go. When we got to our designated marks, we paused for about ten seconds, the sweat just pouring down our faces.

At the tail end of the pre-game routine came the tough part—the high kicks. We lined up arm-in-arm in one single line stretching nearly the entire length of the field. The Dallas Cowboys Cheerleaders were known for that long line of high kicks. We were the Rockettes of football. Every girl on the squad, however, hated those high kicks because they came at the end of a long dance routine and we were already exhausted. Also, the high kick routine is very, very demanding. We had to be as limber as Gumby and as fit as a marathoner in order to pull it off.

And 1-2-3-4, kick, kick, and 2-2-3-4, kick, kick, and 3-2-3-4, kick, kick, kick, kick, kick, kick we counted to ourselves

★

as we kicked straight over the tops of our heads. There were never low kicks. My knee came right next to my ear at the top of the kick and the sole of my boot pointed right to the sky. Just one good high kick could knock the average human being flat on her back and pull muscles she didn't know existed. And there were at least 100 of them. Sometimes a boot came off, or a top came untied, but we kept right on kicking—5, 6, SEV-en, 8 . . ." Toward the end of the routine, everybody was yelling, "Come on! You can do it! It's almost the end. Come on! Let's go! Higher! Higher! We're almost there."

When the music finally ended, we all bowed. The eight minute pre-game performance was over and I was drenched. My mascara had run down my face and my hair was all matted to my head. Then, the music started again and we danced over to the end zone to form a "V" in front of the goalposts. The players came running out through the "V" and after that, the band struck up the national anthem.

I was never happier to hear that great tune. Not out of patriotism, but because for the first time we were able to take a breather. As all of the fans' attention focused on the flag on the other side of the field, I got a chance to wipe the perspiration out of my eyes and rearrange my shorts. After the National Anthem, we pranced off the field to the tune of "If My Friends Could See Me Now."

That day I found out that cheering at a game was a grueling marathon in which we danced for nearly four straight hours. When the performance was over, I was exhausted. Besides our five set routines (the pre-game and one after each quarter), we danced to whatever songs the band played. Whenever there was a time-out, when a player got injured, or during almost any other break in the game, they struck up a tune. We also did routines that weren't set to music,

★

so we were always dancing. At the end of the game when the clock was counting down, I was counting down with it. And when the gun finally went off, I let out a great sigh of relief. Then I dragged my weary body back to the locker room.

After the game I took my clothes off, literally wringing the perspiration out of them. My boots were soaked too. By the end of the game they squished from sweat. Every muscle in my body ached as well—my legs quivered and twitched, my feet throbbed, and my arms felt like I had a barbell in each hand. But I still had a great big smile on my face. I had just experienced the most exhilarating four hours in my life.

I changed slowly back into my warm-ups and tried to freshen up my makeup as best as I could. We all knew the fans would be outside waiting for us, so we had to get our game faces on again with those big Texas smiles.

The game was an eye-opening experience in which I realized how potent the popularity of the Cheerleaders was. But until I came out of the locker room, walked up the ramp, and saw that sea of people waiting for us to emerge, I didn't really know how big we had become. When the first of us came out of the tunnel, the crowd let out such a squeal of excitement that I was scared by their passionate frenzy. Suddenly, we weren't protected by the ten-foot walls that surrounded the field. The fans could get at us. I stepped back for a second. Then I saw the look of awe on the faces of the people and I knew I'd be okay. To most of them, I was like a great singer who had made them feel so wonderful so many times that they just wanted to come up and say, "Thank you!"

I waded right into the crowd and they surrounded me in a loving cocoon. Little girls looked up at me with their

★

mouths open. Grown men were so nervous their hands were shaking as they put their programs in my hands to autograph. Women smiled at me in a way that they rarely smiled at a beautiful woman. There wasn't a hint of jealousy. In their minds I was too far beyond them to be any threat. And when I said, "Hi, how are y'all? My name is Stephanie!" I could see that love in their eyes, like I was an older sister who'd gone off and become a movie star but had never forgotten them.

When I put on the uniform of a Dallas Cowboys Cheerleader, I was transformed into something royal. There was a mystique surrounding the Cheerleaders that created a frenzy wherever we went. People stood in the hot sun for three or four hours to get an autograph from an eighteen-year-old girl who led cheers for a football team; a girl who the day before might have been a waitress who they growled at, "Hey, make it snappy with those French fries, will you, honey!"

When I tried out for the team, I wasn't trying out for some cheerleading squad. I was auditioning to be a celebrity who would be whisked off into a fairy tale for a year. I was going to be a movie star, a beauty queen, and a member of an internationally known dance troupe that toured the world. I was trying out for stardom!

From the day of that game and for the next three years, I was on the same level as any major celebrity. People came up to me in restaurants, recognized me on the street, and mobbed me at personal appearances. When I danced they screamed their voices raw. It was intoxicating and thrilling and completely crazy.

After the game, we signed autographs for over an hour, right up until they turned the stadium lights off. We were good to our fans; they were important to us. Then, two

★

security guards walked each girl over to where her car was parked and made sure she got off safely. The fans were still there in the dark, waving and running alongside the car to get a last glimpse at a Dallas Cowboys Cheerleader as she drove off.

I couldn't wait to do it all again next week.

★

2

Daddy was a dentist when Mother first met him back in 1956 at an engagement party down in Phoenix. The party was for Mother's sorority sister and friend Joanne, who was the daughter of Senator Barry Goldwater.

As soon as Mother saw Daddy standing over by the punch bowl she got a feeling. He was dressed in an all-white suit with a red tie, and was smoking a meerschaum pipe—the quintessential Southern gentleman. The sun was gleaming off of him like a suit of armor. She went right to work to find out who he was. It only took Mother about ten minutes to get a complete dossier on him.

He was Dr. Ken Scholz. A Dentist. A Texan. Serving in the military. Due out in June. Former Little All-American football player. Brilliant guy.

He didn't stand a chance! But then he wasn't supposed to. When she walked over to the punchbowl for a drink, dressed in a tight-fitting, white satin, Oriental-style dress with slits up both sides, he fell like a load of bricks. Before the day was over she dumped the guy that brought her and after batting her eyes at Daddy, wished with all her heart that he would call her for a date. Of course, when she came home talking about another guy, her mother, Mamie, wasn't surprised. Mother had been engaged half a dozen times.

"Fell in and out of love as often as she changed clothes," Mamie would say. "But that's a woman's privilege."

★

It took Daddy six weeks to rake up the nerve to ask Mother out. Shortly after their first date, Mother left with a group of friends to attend a summer session at the University of Hawaii. Daddy was serving in the Air Force at the time, and flew over for Mother's birthday. He stayed in the Officer's Quarters at Fort DeRussy in Honolulu. Mother was so impressed that she dropped all of her courses but Hula and Tahitian Dancing so that they could spend more time together on the beach. Daddy slipped an engagement ring on her finger and asked for her hand in marriage.

They met in May and tied the knot in August.

Eight years later, Mother was standing at the window of their hotel room in San Francisco. Daddy had decided dentistry was not for him and he had just completed his residency in orthopedic surgery. It was just after dawn of the biggest day of our father's life. They were in California because he was taking the second portion of his Orthopedic Surgery Boards. He'd been working for years in anticipation of this day and it had been a struggle for them both.

The sun was just coming up over the Bay, the fog pushing in off the Pacific. And there was Daddy, strutting up and down the hill in front of the hotel getting some exercise between exams, psyching himself up and thinking, "There's nothing they can ask me. There's nothing they can ask. Absolutely nothing they can ask on these goddamned boards that I can't tell them the answer to. Nothing! Not a damn thing!"

A fire was burning within him. Mother was watching him from the hotel window, smiling the whole time. Together there wasn't anything anybody could ask either of them for which they wouldn't have had the answer. That's the way they felt about life. That's the way they felt about each other.

*   *   *

★

DEEP IN THE HEART OF TEXAS

Our father grew up on a cotton farm in Corpus Christi. His parents were poor. They had emigrated from Germany and were builders by trade.

Mother also was raised with very little. But her parents, Mamie, and Daddy Joe had a keen sense of humor, and they used to tell about the time when they went down to visit Mamie's relatives.

"We all lived a hard life. We were common, ordinary people. Not too much education. But so what? We worked hard to get ahead in life. I've always believed money doesn't buy class, but in *Aunt Essie*'s case, it couldn't have hurt.

"When Aunt Essie married *Jim Bob*, Joe and I went down for the ceremony. Now this was a couple that deserved each other, for better or for worse.

"Oh my God, we walked in and I couldn't believe my eyes. They were getting ready to have a big wedding. They had a table in the kitchen with an old oil cloth cover that was darker than the ground out there. On it, they had a gallon jar with mayonnaise. A gallon jar of pickles. The biggest bottle of catsup they could find. The biggest can of peanut butter. I never! All this crap in one corner of the table. 'Just in case you need any of it, see, we got it.' That mayonnaise was never refrigerated. And the dishrag was black as the driveway. Hell, no tellin' how long Aunt Essie had been swipin' with that . . .

"And the bathroom. I couldn't have attempted to scrub that bathtub. More rings than Saturn. And the toilet! If I'd had to stay there I'd said, 'No thank you. I'll just go to the backyard and take a shovel.'

"So we went to a hotel. The next morning they picked us up to take us back to her flea-bitten house. I want you to know I'm not snooty. I can come down to anybody's level. I tried to be one of them. I was sitting at the table that morning

★

with a cup of coffee and Aunt Essie's sister said, 'Would you like a piece of toast?'

" 'Yes, I believe I would.' I was sick to my stomach and I thought that would help settle it. I'm not exaggerating now. I'm sitting at this old table with the filthy oilcloth. And she pitched that piece of toast from the cabinet and it hit that dirty table and slid right across and hit my cup and came to rest right in front of me like a ringer in horseshoes. I wouldn't have eaten that thing if I hadn't had a bite in a winter month . . . The amazing part is they were all healthy as hogs."

That's the way Daddy grew up too. Life was a day-to-day struggle. Daddy was the oldest of three kids and he was expected to get up in the dark every morning and plow the fields and do the chores before he went to school. Then from the time he got back from school until there was no light he picked cotton. It's windy out on the coast in Corpus Christi and he'd come back from a day in the field with his mouth full of dirt. He had to pick it out of his teeth with a toothpick.

His father was against football. But Daddy defied him and went out for football anyway. That's how Daddy got to go to college. He got a football scholarship to Baylor and then moved over to Texas A & I down in Kingsville, where he was a Little All-American halfback. He didn't want to end up being a football coach or back on the farm so he went on to dental school instead of playing professional football. Football had been just a means to an end.

Every day when he was in that field picking that cotton he kept telling himself over and over, "I'm going to get out of this field one day and I'll never go back." That was the source of his maniacal drive to get through college and med

★

school. Everytime he'd think about that cotton, he'd study harder.

"Every step I take in life is going to be farther and farther from that farm," he promised himself as he looked in that rearview mirror at the cotton stretching as far away from him as he could see. And he made good on that promise. The problem was that later, when my father was worth a fortune, he was still looking in that rearview mirror.

Daddy tore through dental school. But then he saw that being a dentist wasn't going to get him where he wanted, so he went to med school and eventually, took a residency in orthopedic surgery. Daddy became a very successful doctor. He was one of the best orthopedic surgeons in Texas and the nation. He invented the Scholz ankle currently in use today for artificial ankle replacements. This made him well known nationally as well as internationally.

Parkland Hospital in Dallas, where JFK was taken after he was shot, was where Daddy trained. In fact, Daddy was supposed to be on call the day Kennedy died. But he switched call assignments with another doctor for that weekend or he would have worked on JFK.

As a resident at Parkland, Daddy's nickname was "Tiger" because he was so aggressive. He was always making deals, anything to get ahead on his measly resident's salary. Daddy had a parking pass card for the gate at Parkland. Without a card, it was twenty-five cents to park. So he'd stand out in the parking lot like he was a lot attendant, take quarters from the people driving up, and let them in with his card— only until he had enough money to go get dinner.

Daddy was very smart. Instead of looking around Dallas for a job with all the other hungry young surgeons, he scoured all of Texas to find his niche. When Daddy interviewed in Lubbock, he knew he had found a sweet deal. There were very few orthopedic men in the whole town.

★

Lubbock was wide open and it turned out to be a gold mine for him.

What distinguished my father from most other doctors was that he was also a great businessman. He belied that old joke about doctors and their investments. He was very shrewd when it came to his money. In fact, he had a kind of disdain for the average doctor.

"You know what they say about doctors," he would tell us. "They drive the biggest cars and live in the biggest houses and their families wear the finest clothes. And they always owe the most money. They die in the operating room with their gloves on trying to dig their way out of debt. That's not my idea of how to live . . .

"Marry a successful businessman," he used to say. "He'll make ten times what a doctor makes and his hours won't be as long."

When Highland Hospital in Lubbock went up for sale, my father tried to get a group of doctors together to buy it. But none of them had the nerve. "I know we can make it," he told them. But they were too frightened. So Daddy scraped and borrowed himself to the hairline and bought the place by himself. "Ken, you're a fool," everyone said. "You can't buy a hospital alone!"

"Watch me!" he said. Then he got to work. The pressure was enormous. Daddy either was going to make Highland Hospital profitable or he was going to go bankrupt.

Luckily, he had a very successful practice so he almost single-handedly kept the hospital full himself. Every time he admitted a patient, he was putting money in his own pocket. He worked fifteen-, eighteen-hour days for eight years and often didn't come home for two or three days at a time. He slept, ate, and worked at Highland.

Then came the time when the megacorporations like Humana, AMI, and Kaiser were buying up little hospitals all

★

across the country. They'd buy the hospitals at any price because each corporation wanted to set up its own network of nationwide medical facilities. And there were only a limited number of existing hospitals to buy. It was a seller's market straight out of a dream. And here was Daddy in Lubbock with a little 123-bed hospital just like they all wanted.

He had a field day with all these guys hungering for his place. He'd haul in one corporation after another with all their lawyers and accountants and deal with them for a couple of weeks or months. And if they didn't give him exactly what he wanted in the contract, he'd send them packing.

AMI had a deal with him and they tried to change one detail in the contract by a quarter of a percent and he told them to get on out of his office.

Then he bumped the price up another two million and called in another group. Finally, he got a group to structure the deal exactly the way he wanted it, so he sold it to them, for twenty times the amount he had paid for it eight years before.

Boom! A grand slam home run!

Daddy closed the deal at a time when interest rates were very high. He took the money and sunk it in tax-free municipal bonds which is not smart unless you figure the interest rates will go down. At the time, the prime rate was above 20 percent. He figured it would never last.

Boom! Two months later the rates plummeted and he multiplied his money. Another grand slam home run!

After that, Daddy bought a Ford dealership in Scottsdale and then he went to Las Vegas and bought a Dollar Rent-a-Car agency. Guess what kind of cars they used? Fords, of course. So he bought Fords from his dealership at a rock bottom price, rented them out for two years, and depreciated them. Then he cleaned them up, sold them back to his used

★

car division cheap, and made another profit from them. It was like a money machine.

Next, Daddy was involved as a principal in the acquisition of Furr's-Bishop's, a national cafeteria chain, from K-Mart. The acquisition became a public traded limited partnership almost a year later and was listed on the N.Y. Stock Exchange.

From a hard-working surgeon to a major player in international financial circles in three years!

While Daddy was making a fortune, Mother was busy putting them at the top of Lubbock society and grooming her three girls. She was the perfect hostess, wife, and mother. She was the lovely veneer.

Ken and Nancy Scholz were an unstoppable team. World-beaters. They'd fly their Lear jet into Vegas and Daddy would walk through Caesar's wearing his silver and blue ostrich-skin boots—with a silver star and his name inlaid on the sides—a diamond-studded gold-nugget belt buckle, and a Rolex watch. Mother was the perfect complement with her floor-length sable and fifty grand in diamonds. The three of us would stroll behind, decked out in our latest Bob Mackie evening gowns. People would turn their heads. "I recognize them. Now, what are their names?" We felt like movie stars.

Together there was nothing, absolutely nothing, we couldn't conquer. Nothing!

★

3

Lubbock, Texas, where we were born and raised, is cotton country, and therefore, its history is steeped in slavery. General Lubbock was the first confederate governor of Texas. He stood up to the Yankees when Sam Houston tried to talk some sense into Texans about how a civil war would only devastate Texas. Houston was right, of course, but Lubbock was the hero and when it was all done they named this patch of cotton fields after him.

When you fly into Lubbock all you see is the brown-red dirt and the dusty-green cotton plants with their white balls of cotton. All three of us girls entered "Maid of Cotton," and during the pageant everything we wore, of course, had to be made of 100 percent . . . well, you get it.

Lubbock is perfectly flat; a big pile of cow paddies is the biggest hill you'll ever see. It's also a one-story town. You can stand on your roof and yell to your neighbor ten blocks away, that is, if the wind blowing in off the plains doesn't blow you off your roof. The wind also dries out the cotton fields and big clouds of manure dust swirl up in the air and . . . ooooh, what a stench! You can barely breathe and what you do breathe is really awful. At school, many of the kids wore scarves across their faces like the old cowboys riding drag in a cattle drive to survive the dust storms. You didn't dare curl your hair, because if you did, by the time you got to class you were whipped senseless.

★

Lubbock sits in the Texas panhandle, smack in the middle of the tornado belt. From time to time the town gets wiped out. There was one long block of houses in particular that tornadoes destroyed several times, so they finally decided to build them underground. It's funny to drive down the street and see only a long row of vacant lots with the mailboxes sticking up out of the ground. No windows or doors, just mailboxes.

Still, Lubbock is a great place to live because of its people. The wind can be freezing but you will always stay warm because of your neighbors. Even the storekeepers are your best friends. If they don't have what you want, they tell you where to get it.

In Lubbock everybody knows everybody else. Sometimes that was the problem of living in a small town. Everyone knew everything that happened to us, good or bad, practically before we did. Luckily, nothing that big ever happened in Lubbock.

Being a Baptist town, there's no drinking allowed in Lubbock. If you want some liquor you've got to drive out to "The Strip," a little unpaved road directly across the street from the Lubbock city limits. The Strip is lined with six or seven liquor stores and nothing else. Just liquor stores.

They don't condone dancing in Lubbock though. In fact, when Suzette became a Cowboys Cheerleader, she went to go to the pastor and asked him if it was okay if she danced for the team. "Honey," he said, "you can dance all you like for the Dallas Cowboys. It's those other cowboys we want you to stay away from."

That's what life is like in Lubbock, nothing much to do except dream. And the dream of every little girl in town—in the whole state of Texas—is to join the Dallas Cowboys Cheerleaders or become Miss America, which are about the same thing.

★

DEEP IN THE HEART OF TEXAS

*   *   *

When we were growing up, the State Finals of The Imperial Miss America Beauty Pageant in Houston was the focal point of every summer. Back then, our lives revolved around beauty pageants. We weren't "pageant girls"; we didn't go to every pageant in the Southwest like some of them and we didn't die if we lost. But the pageant became a sort of final exam in our education as Southern Ladies. That's what Mother and Mamie were—Southern Ladies in the finest tradition. And so were Great-grandma and Granny Valentine before them. That's what Mother brought us up to be as well.

Mother had a Master Plan. She waged a kind of war against slovenly dress, bad manners, foul language, and anything else that wasn't fit for a lady. And no general ever carried out his plan of attack with more precision and tenacity than Mother. She had a goal for us. And every step was carefully calculated along the way from kindergarten until we were grown. She took nothing for granted and left nothing to chance.

One year Mother decided we were going to fly to a pageant in Amarillo. So she went to work making arrangements. Southwest Airlines had just started service to Lubbock airport and she was unfamiliar with their aircraft. So Mother called the company to find out how the plane would accommodate our luggage. Luggage is the number one priority of a traveling lady—inside are the tools of her trade, the magic props that transform her into a gorgeous woman. Mother needed to know how many costumes she could carry on board and how many she'd have to check in. Southwest answered with some song and dance about "every plane is different." So Mother figured she'd have to somehow get on board that plane and check it out for herself. It was the only way.

★

With a little work, it wasn't long before she hit on the perfect scheme. We had a cousin who had had a recent operation on his arm and was flying back to Amarillo. He pretended he was just about ready to expire and needed help getting onto the plane. Mother escorted him on board, and once there, went to work checking out the overhead bins, opening the hangup closets, and looking under the seats for this and that.

The problem however, was they were the last to get on board and her cousin's seat was way in the back. She didn't have a lot of time to look. Southwest is the quintessential commuter airline—it's like a bus pulling up to the curb, loading up passengers, shutting the doors, and leaving for Amarillo. And as Mother is checking out the overhead bins, they slam the door and start to taxi. Now it happens to be St. Patrick's Day and, of course, Mother is dressed in all green—very, very bright green—green dress, green shoes, green bag, green pearls, green sunglasses, green earrings, and green eye shadow.

Feeling the plane move, she starts running up the aisle. "Excuse me! Excuse me! Excuse me, Miss! Miss? Honey, y'all are going to have to turn the plane around."

"Ma'am, please take a seat."

"I'm sorry but there's been a mistake." And she starts knocking on the cockpit door.

A second later the co-pilot sticks his head out. "What's the problem, lady?"

"Excuse me sir, but I'm not supposed to be on this plane. Would you mind backing up and dropping me off at the gate again?"

"Lady, we can't just turn this baby around."

"Captain, I escorted my seriously ill cousin on board and they've shut the door before I could get off." And she flashes

★

him that million-dollar smile, reads his name tag, and puts
her hand ever so softly on his arm and almost whispers,
"Can't you please help me, Larry."

My mother has the most beautiful violet eyes you've ever
seen. They could melt a suit of armor at twenty paces. She
bats her foot-long lashes a couple of times, her eyes get
moony and poor Larry doesn't stand a chance.

He is looking at her, taking in the whole dazzling picture.
The hair is swooped up in those blonde curls, the makeup
applied like an artist. Then his eyes are pulled down to that
figure. Not an ounce of fat anywhere except where it counts,
long slender dancer's legs, and a pair of full breathtaking
breasts staring him in the face. But fooling a man is easier
than convincing a four-year-old about Santa. A one-hundred-
dollar dye job, a couple thousand dollars' worth of makeup
on your vanity, and weekly worship services at Neiman's.
And, sweetheart, it's like ringing the dinner bell at Pavlov's
house.

The pilot's mouth takes on an uncontrollable smile. "Ah,
why not? It's St. Patrick's Day, right?"

"Oh, thank you, Larry. You are the nicest man!"

"No problem at all, ma'am."

He closes the door and mother gets that look of tri-
umph in her eyes she always gets when she's won another
battle for Southern femininity. Like she always told us,
"A lady always gets her way if she does it with class and
style."

But mother's got one more hurdle before she's through.
The plane pulls up to the terminal and an accordion gate is
rolled out for her, but the plane is a little cock-eyed coming
in so it doesn't quite fit snug. There's about a two foot gap
between the plane and the gate. No problem. Mother backs
up into the galley and takes a running leap in those four-

★

inch green spikes and jumps into the waiting arms of the gate agent.

Mission accomplished!

Most of the time we drove to pageants. The feat there was packing four females into a little bitty full-size station wagon that could only hold nine linebackers. Mother was notorious for her packing. Even if we were only going overnight to Ballinger, Texas, she'd take along ten bags.

When we were going to pageants it was worse, of course. Fifteen jumbo Samsonites were a minimum if we really stuffed them full. On top of that, Suzette's "talent" was usually gymnastics. When she was a Cowboys Cheerleader they called her "Flipper" because she could do flips head-over-heels the entire length of Texas Stadium. At pageants she'd do a few flips and then she'd flip up on the balance beam. So when we packed we usually had to wrestle that four-by-four up onto the top of the station wagon.

We all had to help get it up there because Daddy was never around. We learned early in life that if your daddy is a doctor, you don't see him much. But it didn't bother us a lot because we were so proud of him. And also, with Mother keeping us so busy with dance lessons and singing lessons and piano lessons and tennis lessons and getting ready for this play and that pageant, who had time to miss him?

We were experts at tying the beam down, then loading about ten more suitcases on top of that and ten more in the back of the wagon. And off we'd go—Mother, Suzette, Sheri, and me and sometimes even Mamie. Off we'd go to Waco or Amarillo or El Paso, off to win Cinderella Girl or Imperial Miss Texas or Little Miss.

This time, however, we were going to the big one. The National Finals of the Imperial Miss Pageant in Houston,

★

DEEP IN THE HEART OF TEXAS

Texas. This was a very exciting trip for us because we were all competing and we knew we were going to win. We'd all been working very hard and were very confident.

"We want to win everything this year, Mother!" Suzette said.

"Now girls, remember it's inner beauty that counts most. Not winning. Beauty comes from within. You're only as pretty as you are inside."

We'd heard this little speech daily since we could walk. And we all believed it too, but we had a mission to accomplish. "Okay, okay, Mother, we'll be beautiful inside but we're going to beat the pants off everybody at that pageant this year!"

"Stephanie!" Mother looked at me very sternly for a second but then she smiled and started laughing with all of us. "All right. Let's go get 'em girls." And she threw that Olds into gear and off we went.

On these long drives to pageants, mother usually spent a lot of time instructing us on the finer points of how to be a true Southern Lady. We enjoyed these talks because we wanted to be Southern Ladies too—like Mother and Mamie. We knew the recipe by heart.

"Now a lady never raises her voice. A man doesn't like a shrill woman. Not for his wife. You can get as mad as you want at me, girls. But you wait until we get back to our hotel room to let it out because if you act like a brat around the hotel, it'll hurt you no matter how lovely you are on stage. A judge might be down in the lobby just when you start screaming."

"We know, Mother."

"And no matter what you do, do not go swimming."

"Mother! No swimming? It's boiling in Houston!"

"I don't care how hot it gets. If you come out of that pool with your hair all dripping, there's no telling what a judge might think."

★

"Mother!"

"You want to win, don't you?"

"You bet!"

"Okay. No swimming."

"Yes, mother."

We drove for a while longer and then she remembered something else.

"And another thing. Keep an eye on your things. I want everything that you're going to wear the next day laid out on the dresser before you go to bed."

"We know Mother."

Mother always had us check and recheck everything the night before a competition to make sure things were just right—the shoes, the bows, the hose, everything. This was one of her strict rules. And we understood why and complied with it like it was life or death.

A beauty pageant is a competition. And girls can get vicious when it comes to seeing who's the most beautiful. The wicked Queen was ready to kill when her "mirror mirror on the wall" gave the wrong answer. That might have been a fairy tale, but it was based on real life. There have been incidents where one contestant has cut another's dress the night before a pageant, and when she puts it on the night of the evening dress competition, there's only one strap left. Or one shoe is taken so the favored girl has to clomp out in her red dress with *beige* pumps, which stands out like a hog at a turkey trot.

A beauty pageant can become a ferocious battle between females; something that nobody likes to admit, even though it's true. A good-looking girl has a huge advantage in nearly everything she does. That's why other women might set their sights on undermining her from the moment she's noticed. If Mother Teresa was a knockout, they'd hate her too.

A beauty pageant can be a tremendous help for a girl. If

★

you think the girls at pageants are a bunch of bubble brains, think again. The truth is, most pageant contestants are go-getters. They learn how to compete and how to use every-thing at their disposal to win. This is the advantage little boys get over little girls. It's not that they learn to play sports and we don't, it's that they learn to compete. Most women who learn to compete well at pageants do very well in the social and business worlds. A beauty pageant prepares girls for the grueling, back-stabbing, dog-eat-dog competi-tion of daily life.

We drove all day to get to Houston, stopping for gas and food along the way. Before we got to the hotel, we made, as always, "The Final Stop." We pulled into a gas station, piled out, and commandeered the Ladies Room. We changed our clothes, put on our makeup and did our hair. When we walked into the pageant hotel we had to look gorgeous, and nothing short of perfection would do. We had to look like we'd just taken a break at the Cotillion Ball, not like we had spent the last eight or nine hours stuffed in the back of a station wagon with ten suitcases.

The Final Stop, of course, would take at least a good hour—running back and forth to the car to get this and that, plugging in blow dryers, yelling out instructions to the next sister waiting in line outside the restroom door. "Sheri! Please, get my pink socks. Not the ones with the lace ruffles. The ones with the roses on the sides."

Of course, this would sometimes try the patience of the gas guys, but we'd just ladle on the charm and they'd melt into a male puddle like the grease stains under their filthy old cars. By the time we'd leave, looking like a carload of Miss Americas waving and smiling and blowing them kisses, they felt like a couple of Rolls Royces with their engines

★

revving at a million rpms, instead of just a couple of greasy old jalopies.

Then we'd all be off to the pageant hotel where mother— looking like a million, the charm on her megawatt personality turned up to melt—would lead us single file into the lobby. Behind us a fleet of bell boys would be unloading the wagon. The other girls would be arriving frowzy and grouchy, popping gum and dressed like joggers, but the Scholz girls would march in with their shoulders back, hair poufed out, makeup perfect. We looked sensational.

In the lobby, Mother would be here and there, friendly as a preacher. Never screechy, though. Always a lady. That was another thing she taught us. A lady is never screechy. Whenever Mother walked into a room it lit up. Everybody knew she was there. That was one of her goals for the evening, to walk in the place and have the whole room turn and stare. But you never heard her. (Unless, of course, she was on stage. "Then it's okay to be as loud as you want, girls.") You might sometimes overhear her talking with someone. But only if you were right next to her.

That was Mother's secret. She exploded into a room without a sound. That's how a real lady did it. A low-class gutter sow can be heard during a touchdown at a sports saloon. It doesn't matter if she's decked out in diamonds and Chanel, she's a tramp. "A lady is as quiet and beautiful as a rose opening in the morning." That's what Mother always told us.

Early the next morning in Houston the phone rang and Mother answered.

"Don't panic, Nancy. This is *Gene*. . . ."

Gene was the director of the pageant.

". . . there's a fire in the hotel."

★

DEEP IN THE HEART OF TEXAS

We had heard some alarms going off but we were dressing to go down to interview with the judges, so we ignored them. We were too busy dolling up Sheri, who was first up.

". . . now this is what you're supposed to do . . . ," Gene went on.

Mother, of course, was panic stricken. We were standing there half-dressed with our hair in curlers. Mother was in high heels, hose, a slip, and a bra.

". . . go to the door and try the door handle. If it's not hot, open the door. Take some blankets, wet them down. If the hallway is filled with smoke, get down on your hands and knees, put the blankets over you and crawl to your left to the elevator."

"No," Mother said. "You're never supposed to get in an elevator during a fire."

"Go to the elevator. The firemen will be waiting for you."

"I'd rather go down the stairs."

"No," Gene insisted. "There are very few people left up there. Do as we say. The elevator is working. The firemen will be there."

Well, of course, Mother was petrified but she never let on to us kids.

"Well, we've got a little problem girls," she said while she was ripping the covers off all the beds.

"Mother! What are you doing? My dress!"

"Girls, there's a little fire in the hotel."

Then she took Suzette off to one side. "Suzette, you're the oldest. There's a fire in the hotel. There's no problem. We're just going to have to crawl down the hall to the elevator. The firemen are waiting there."

Suzette looked at her and went into a complete panic.

"If we're going to the lobby, Sheri needs her party dress on. The judges could be down there."

★

"Suzette, honey, don't worry about that. Put something on her to get her out of here."

So Suzette turned around and proceeded to doll Sheri up anyway. The hotel was burning down and Suzette was calmly putting the finishing touches on her little sister. Curling her hair with an iron and combing it out.

"Stephanie! Put your robe on!" Mother screamed.

"No way I'm going out there in my robe. I might as well throw that crown out the window." And I started putting on a dress and pulling the curlers out of my hair. This all took about five minutes during which time Mother threw her hands in the air and started helping me comb my hair out.

Finally, we were ready to go out the door. Mother came out of the bathroom with three dripping blankets.

"No way Mother! It'll ruin our dresses. We'll take our chances."

She saw right away it was hopeless to try to talk us under those wet rags so she just dropped them right there on the floor. We opened up the door and the smoke wasn't that bad so we didn't need the wet blankets anyway. We all got down on our hands and knees and started crawling along the hallway with Sheri in front in this fluffy party dress.

"I can't crawl in this dress," Sheri said. So Mother put her on her back horse-back style and kept on crawling.

We finally got to the elevator and there were the firemen. We stepped on the elevator and were all so thankful that we had made it.

"Oh, thank you," Mother said. "I thought we were all going to die back there."

One of the firemen slammed the door shut quickly and pushed the button for the lobby.

*   *   *

★

DEEP IN THE HEART OF TEXAS

The next day was even more eventful with a murder on the floor above us and a kidnap attempt on Sheri.

Mother was sitting with Sheri downstairs in the restaurant when a strange man walked by, giving Sheri a serious eye. At the time, Mother didn't think much about it. Over the next few days this man kept popping up here and there eyeing Sheri. But still Mother didn't worry about it because Sheri was glued to her side most of the time.

A couple of nights after the fire, Sheri wanted to go down the hall to the Coke machine to get a soda. Mother didn't want her to go by herself so four little pageant girls next door who were about twelve said they'd take her.

Mother stayed in the room as they all walked down the hall. When they turned the corner a man was standing there against the wall.

"Hi, Sheri, honey. How are you?" he said.

"I'm fine, sir. How are you?"

"Just fine. Where are y'all going?" he said and reached out to take Sheri's hand.

That's when the four girls sensed something wasn't right. There was a stairway "Exit" door right behind them so they grabbed Sheri and shoved her through and ran up the stairs. Then they ran up to the next floor. They could hear the man slamming the door behind him and stomping up the stairs after them.

They ran halfway down the hall until they saw a utility room and they hid in there with the brooms and mops until he went by. Then they snuck out and ran back down the stairs. When they finally shoved Sheri in the door they were all bawling their heads off, hysterical.

"He tried to take Sheri! He tried to take Sheri!"

"Who did?"

"A man."

"What man?"

★

"We don't know. He was just standing there."

Mother grabbed Sheri and the four girls and marched right down to the front desk and told them what happened. But the people behind the desk just looked at her, whispered between themselves, and then made a call.

"Mrs. Scholz would you please take a seat over there."

"Hey, what's going on?"

"Please take a seat. A police detective will be right down to talk with you."

A few minutes later a couple of plainclothes detectives came down and showed their badges to Mother.

"Okay. What's going on," Mother demanded. "Somebody is trying to kidnap my baby. But nobody will tell me anything."

When she said this the police came clean. The Chief of Detectives pulled Mother aside.

"Look, Mrs. Scholz, the truth is we're having a problem. Your daughter could be in danger. There's been what appears to be a murder upstairs and we think the two incidents are related. A man has been killed over a drug deal. We think the man who tried to take your daughter is one of the drug dealers staying in a room above you. We don't want to arrest him until we find out what's going on. You'll need a guard on your daughter at all times."

"Well," Mother said, "that's enough! I'm taking my daughters out of here this instant."

That's when the pageant director, Gene, tried to stop her.

"Nancy, won't you please reconsider? If you stay you will be provided with a 24-hour, round-the-clock escort. And there will be a guard stationed in the hall outside your door."

"Absolutely not! First there's a fire, then somebody tries to kidnap my baby, and now they tell me somebody's been murdered. I'm not staying here another second with my daughters."

★

When she got back to the room she explained the situation to the three of us.

"Pack your things," she said. "We're getting out of here!"

"No way, Mother!" we all shouted. "We're staying! We're gonna win this pageant!"

We'd worked our little fannies off all year for this. We wanted to win those trophies!

And we did do just that. We cleaned up. Suzette won first runner-up in the Queen's division and was chosen Miss Congeniality. I won the Empress division. And Sheri won the Countess division. But Mother really took the cake by winning Talent for the mothers with her eye-catching tap dance routine to "There's No Business Like Show Business."

Mother may have reached the zenith of her planning when she took Sheri to the Miss Teen U.S.A. pageant. By then, Daddy had sold the hospital, so Mother had all the money she needed to really implement her strategies. The pageant organizers had sent out a questionnaire to all the contestants. One of the things they wanted to know was what airline and flight the contestants would arrive on, and how they would get from the airport to the pageant hotel. Mother informed them that she and Sheri would be coming in on their own private jet and a limo would ferry them to the hotel.

That started a stir that reverberated throughout the pageant. When Sheri and my mother arrived at the hotel, it fulfilled everyone's fantasy about Texas. Mother was dressed in daffodil yellow from hat to shoes and Sheri was at her side in a dazzling watermelon number. It was a sight to behold.

The New York Times thought so. "Miss Teen Texas arrived at this first-ever Miss Teen U.S.A. pageant in her own Lear jet, no less," the Times reporter gushed.

Richard Guy and Rex Holt had managed to groom girls

★

to win an unprecedented five Miss U.S.A. crowns in a row—all of them from Texas. Texas had a bigger than life reputation in pageant circles, as well as everywhere else. To top it all, Sheri was a Guy-Réx protégé. They had guided her from an early age, softened up her hair, got rid of her favorite blue eyeshadow, and designed all her clothes. Inside the fourteen suitcases that followed Mother and Sheri into the hotel were matching outfits for every single day—every luncheon, every rehearsal, every photo session, every handshake with any dignitary that paraded by them. Every outfit was a complete coordinated ensemble with matching bag, shoes, and hair ribbons. Every bit of it was handmade and designed by the famous Guy-Réx pageant experts. Sheri even had a very special costume to represent the great state of Texas—a gold lamé cowgirl outfit cut down to her navel with gold lamé boots, hat, and fringe vest to match.

The whole place was buzzing.

Sheri was living the fantasy of every little girl in the world who ever played with a Barbie doll. It was dress-up every day in the most fanciful of outfits at the most glamorous of any adolescent female event—the Miss Teen U.S.A. contest.

Mother knew exactly how to make every little girl's dream come true.

★

4

When you meet our mother, you know instantly how we got to be the way we are. See . . . Mother is a little eccentric.

Mother's big obsession was always her hair. When she was a little girl she could never get it to do what she wanted. So she swore if she could ever afford it she'd go to the hairdresser every day. And that's what she did. Rain or shine, she'd drop us off at school and head for the hairdresser. When she emerged an hour later, she was ready to conquer the world—or at least Lubbock.

Mother was always a raven-haired beauty. One day she drove us to school, dropped us off, kissed us good-bye, and when she picked us up that afternoon she was a platinum blonde. She also had the only wig closet in Lubbock. There were wigs of every shape, cut, and color imaginable lined up on the shelves.

Looking good was very important to mother. She took two or three baths a day in order to have that fresh look all the time. She was always perfectly dressed and perfectly groomed. Mother would take tennis lessons but she never wanted to play because she didn't want to get dirty and sweaty. She always had the snazziest togs. She'd go on ski trips complete with the fur and the outfit, but she'd never see a slope. Instead, she'd go for a drive or go shopping and come back later saying, "Oh, I had such a great day on those slopes."

★

Mother would refuse to go to the mailbox ten steps from our door unless she was impeccably dressed and in full makeup. And she wouldn't allow us to either.

We were taught to always put the right clothes with the right accessories; everything had to go together. I would come home from school and there would be a dress on the bed along with matching shoes, hose, purse, fingernail polish, and lipstick.

We were never allowed to wear blue jeans—even for climbing trees. Finally we had to buy our own and hide them in the back of Suzette's car. We'd drive around the corner, run into the filling station, wiggle into our blue jeans, and off we'd go. Eventually, after we begged her for months, Mother broke down and let us wear them. But if they had gold stitching, we had to wear a gold shirt to match.

Everything I ever wore matched. I still match to this day because it was the way I was dressed growing up. Just about every day I'll go somewhere and people will get that look on their face when they see me with the peach shoes, peach dress, peach bag, and peach earrings and lipstick.

"Oh, don't worry," I tell them. "I was brought up this way. I can't help myself." That usually gets a big laugh of recognition.

To this day I tend to dress like my mother. I like to call it "creative." I guess I knew I'd reached the peak of my creativity when I was getting into the car to go shopping one afternoon and the nice old lady down the block asked me if I was going to a costume party.

Mother lived for the night because that's when she could dress up and get fancy. If it was her choice, she'd go out every single night. The perfect evening for her would be to go to the Lubbock Club for an elegant dinner and then go dancing until three or four in the morning. She never really went out for the meal itself, she just liked to get gussied up

★

in her baubles and beads, waltz into a restaurant, take in the beauty of the decor, and stir her food around. What she had really come for, what she couldn't wait to do, was to get out on the dance floor. Mother will still dance anything you want to dance—rock'n'roll, swing, waltz. She can do it all. And 99 times out of 100 she'll be the best dancer there. Unless, of course, there's another trained professional dancer at the party.

During the day, Mother chauffeured us to dance lessons in her lavender Cadillac with white leather seats and spoke wheels. "It's a full-time job to groom a girl, especially three girls." She took us to school every day and when she'd pick us up afterward she'd have a snack in the car for us. Then we'd be off to the dance studio, where we would take three or four dance classes in a day. The school bell would ring at 3:30 and it would start—3:45 to 4:30 tap, 4:30 to 5:30 ballet, 5:30 to 6:30 jazz, 6:30 to 7:30 break to go to the Dairy Queen, and 7:30 to 8:30 twirling, voice, or acting.

After it was all over we'd go home, study, and go to bed. It was our life. No wonder we seldom got in trouble. There was never any time.

We were always achieving. We never rested. There was always this pressure from within to do things bigger and better. We were always in competitions. And a lot of the time we won. But if we didn't, we never dwelled on it. There was no time. We were already off to the next thing Mother had us signed up for.

My mother was the greatest mom in the world for three little girls growing up in Texas. She loved the world of imagination, to have dreams and to see us dream. But she also knew how to make those dreams come true.

We called her "The Coach." She was always there for us. She was always getting us the right dance instructor or

★

helping us to prepare for a speech or quizzing us for an exam. She always saw ahead. If there were cheerleader tryouts coming up in five months, she made us work hard on the gymnastics stunts that we'd be using in the tryouts.

The junior high school play was very important to every ninth grader. When Suzette was in the ninth grade her class was going to put on "Oklahoma." So, of course, she wanted to try out. But Suzette knew she couldn't sing her way out of a paper bag, so she figured if she got really lucky she might get a part in the chorus.

"Mother," Suzette said when she got home, "the tryouts are coming up for the play at school."

"I know, honey. I got the sheet music for Oklahoma right here. We'll get you ready."

"But I can't sing."

"Let me tell you, Suzette, those other little girls trying out have had no training in stage work. They're going to stand up there like a bunch of little Minnie Mouses and sing in their sweet little voices. When they hand you the mike, I want you to belt it out and move. This is a musical. Stage presence is probably more important than singing."

Mother then set her up with a fabulous vocal teacher named Inez Farrel. They had several weeks to get ready and they worked nearly every night until Suzette sounded pretty good. When the big day came, Suzette tried out and afterwards she thought, "Boy, I bet I did pretty good." But the next day, they posted everyone's name who made the cast except the four main leads. There was no Suzette Scholz in sight. Poor Suzette was devastated. She came home crying. Everyone was going to be in it, all of her friends. And she was going to be watching out in the audience.

The next day she got called into the choir room and was told she had gotten the main lead as Laurie. She nearly

★

fainted. The next year when I tried out for the lead in "Where's Charley?" it was the same story. Mother groomed me and I got the part.

When Sheri's turn came, Mother groomed her too. To help Suzette and me succeed, Mother had tapped into our tenacious personalities. Sheri was more serene, but also the most beautiful and the most versatile of the three of us. Mother helped Sheri use talent and beauty rather than a competitive spirit to achieve her goals and this worked well. Sheri became Varsity cheerleader at Mackenzie Junior High and Coronado High School and she has an entire roomful of pageant trophies, including 1983–84 Miss Texas Teen U.S.A.

The most important social function in a Texas community is the football game on Friday night when two towns meet head on. And the most important competition of every school year in Texas is for cheerleader. The cheerleader represents not just the school but the entire community. Becoming a cheerleader was a very big deal not just for the girl but for her entire family.

When we were cheerleaders, everyone in town knew us. We were little celebrities.

"Hi, Suzette. How are you?" people would call out.

"Fine. How are you?"

Then we'd pass five minutes with the person, talking about the football players and school and Mother, without having a clue as to who the person was.

There were always more tears shed over not being elected as a cheerleader than over losing the student body president election. There was also the chance that a parent would challenge the results of cheerleader tryouts, call for a recount, or call for the ouster of the principal. It sounds ridiculous, but at MacKenzie Junior High where Suzette, Sheri, and I all went to school, one parent made such a stink when

★

her daughter didn't win a spot on the cheerleading squad that they had to switch the principal to another school to calm the mother down.

Recently, in a school near Houston, a mother whose daughter was getting ready to try out for high school cheerleader allegedly put out a contract to kill the mother of her daughter's major competitor. Supposedly, the thinking was that overcome by grief the competitor would be less of a threat, and maybe, wouldn't even show up for tryouts at all.

When Suzette was in the ninth grade, Mother got her ready for the approaching cheerleader tryouts. Suzette was still shy back then and cheerleader competition was, and still is, a popularity contest. The most popular and outgoing girls usually win, so mother worked on a different angle. She developed a routine that emphasized Suzette's gymnastic ability. Mother figured nobody else could do flips across the entire length of the stage like Suzette, so she was sure to be selected. Mother was right.

Well, winning cheerleader changed Suzette's life. She went from a shy, sweet child to a very popular, outgoing girl whom everyone knew. And it happened almost overnight, at a very crucial time in her life, too. The girls who go on to become the heads of student council, senior high cheerleaders, Homecoming Queens, and all the rest in high school were almost all junior high cheerleaders. It not only builds your confidence but suddenly everyone in town knows who you are.

When Suzette came out of her cocoon, she was like the beautiful butterfly emerging—fluttering and dancing all over. Today, you can't keep Suzette down. She is the most energetic, positive person on earth, impossible to contain in a room. Her energy level is unbelievable. She literally dances when she talks to you, knocking things over because she's so animated.

★

DEEP IN THE HEART OF TEXAS

When Suzette was a Cowboys Cheerleader, she'd cheer at a game, stay up all night studying, take a test the next morning, then do a charity appearance that night. Everybody would get a kick out of watching Suzette because she put so much into every dance. We all thought she was going to drop dead from a heart attack right there on the field. The girls would tease her, "Suzette, calm down! You're making us all work too hard. We look like we're dogging it next to you."

When Daddy wanted to put a swimming pool in our backyard, mother vetoed him. He already had installed a putting green for golf on one side of the yard. We needed the other side for practicing cheerleading stunts, not for swimming. Besides, Mother wanted us to hold the workouts for cheerleader out there. She knew that if we held practices at our house, she could give us special tips after everyone went home. And she could keep an eye out for any personality problems that might be brewing among the girls in the group. See, Mother was very sensitive to jealousy and how it can destroy a young girl because she had gone through it herself.

When she was a young girl growing up in Roswell, the other girls turned on her because she was pretty and very popular with the boys. There was a picnic one Saturday and a couple of little girls started telling all the boys that Mother had stuffed her bra with socks. Mother didn't need socks in her bra, but after that the little boys were not so nice to her because they equated bra stuffing with forwardness. And little boys, like big boys, are very uncomfortable when they aren't doing all the chasing.

Anyway, the big formal dance was the following week and none of the boys would ask Mother out. She was sitting on her porch crying her eyes out when her neighbor, Robert, who was the star of the high school football team came by.

★

"What are you crying about?" he said.

"I don't have an escort to the dance."

"Well, don't worry about it. I'll take you to that dance."

Mother was in heaven. The star of the football team and he was going to take her. Mamie did all of Mother's sewing and made her a gorgeous formal dress. Mother showed up looking like the Belle of the Ball on the arm of the prize catch in school. That only inflamed the jealousy. One of the girls put her foot on the train of Mother's dress and when she turned and walked off, the whole dress tore off her. There she stood with just a thin petticoat on.

"Get your skirt," Robert said. "Hold it up, and we'll go home. But we'll be right back," he said in a loud voice so all the other girls could hear.

So he took her home and told Mamie, "Take her in and sew that dress back on her. I don't care how you do it. We're going back to that dance."

When Robert got back in the car with Mother he leaned toward her. "Nancy, I want to tell you something. Don't ever let anyone intimidate you. Pick yourself up and go back in there with your head high, with a smile on your face. That's the way you handle people. Don't let them get to you. You're with me now. No one is going to step on your dress again." So Mother was always very aware of jealousy when we were growing up. My father wanted to buy her a Rolls Royce, but she refused. She didn't want people to think she was a snob.

Mother did as much to ensure our popularity as she did to make us succeed at other things because she saw popularity as a way to happiness. Her golden rule was always "Be sweet to everyone." Whether it's a doorman or the garbage man or the maid, they should be treated just like the town big shots. "At school be nice to the thugs and the girls who aren't so popular," she'd instruct us. "You don't have to like what they do, but be nice to them. Now, you don't do it for the votes. You do it because they're humans too. But in the end, it will all come back to you."

As usual, Mother was right. The underdogs and thugs and the people we were nice to ended up voting us in as cheerleaders in junior high and high school, just about every year.

Mamie would also say, "Girls, your mother and I didn't fall off the back of a cantaloupe truck yesterday. Listen to us, because it won't be your best friends that will vote for you." Words of wisdom that rang true.

★

5

Usually, it's only one parent in a family that is the pusher and the motivator. But both Mother and Daddy were overachievers. Both were high-strung, highly motivated, and both very successful. We followed right in their footsteps.

It was always a whirlwind around our house, but whenever we wanted a break we knew we could go to Mamie's house. Mamie was our maternal grandmother and she indulged us as only a grandmother can.

Mamie was our best friend and we spent one night over at her house many weekends from birth right through high school. It was like a hotel. The bedcovers would be pulled back and there were always little treats on the bed.

"Okay," she'd say, "you can go through my purses and whoever finds the most money can keep it all." And she always left lots of change in her purse on purpose.

Mamie's backyard was Fantasyland. It had a huge weeping willow that canopied most of the yard and we just about lived in it. We played back there for hours. Mamie didn't care if we ever went to school either. And a lot of times we didn't when we stayed at her house.

"Well, I guess I'm gonna let you sleep in late today. Now what do you want to do? Eat ice cream or go roller skating?"

Mamie would always join in with us no matter what we did. When we went roller skating, she'd put on a pair of roller skates and go with us. If we'd be giggling about the

★

little boys we liked, Mamie would say, "Well, let's go over and pick up the boys and take 'em out for pizza." And we'd go around and pick them up.

At night we'd all pile into her big poster bed, snuggle under the covers with Mamie and she would tell us about our family, about where we came from. Mamie was also a great story-teller:

My grandparents came from Alabama after the slaves were freed. Grandfather Rayburn owned a bunch of slaves and this couple wanted to come to Texas with them. Eventually, seven families in seven covered wagons started out, including three black families.

The sad part was that most of 'em died several years later in the flu epidemic that hit Texas back in the eighties and nineties when so many people died. Whole towns were wiped out. Lord, it was like the plague in the Dark Ages.

Anyway, they all packed up in the back of these covered wagons. There were no highways, no roads, no nothin'.

I asked Grandma Rayburn, "How in the world did you travel in those covered wagons with all those kids? All hot and dirty. Didn't it nearly drive you crazy?"

"Oh," she said, "we'd stop and find a river and get out and bathe and such."

Like it was nothin'.

Grandma was married when she was fourteen. What a woman. You talk about a strong Texas woman. She was it. Valentine Rayburn. Born on Valentine's Day. Called her Tiny for short.

She had twelve kids, nine of 'em boys. Imagine nine lit-tle boys! Good Lord, what a nightmare! There wasn't a day that went by that there wasn't a broken window or bone. When World War I come along, five of 'em enlisted in one day. They all went down to the train station in Bal-

★

linger to leave on this fruit train and the whole family
went down there in wagons and buggies to see them off.

Uncle Carl was down there at the station saying good-
bye and someone said, "Valentine's got five boys on that
train."

"Yeah," Carl said, "and with her damn luck all five'll
come back."

Grandma Valentine was special. In her lifetime I couldn't
tell you how many children she raised. Nieces and nephews
and grandchildren and what have you. She took anybody
that was homeless. She had the twelve kids of her own,
then she took two children who had lost their parents, relatives of her brother.

She raised black kids, white kids. As long as they were
kids and they were homeless, she raised 'em. She took the
black boy Eddie whose parents had died of the flu and
raised him along with her own kids. In fact, he took the
Rayburn name. Eddie Rayburn. It made no difference to
Granny what the neighbors thought. That boy was hers. A
child was a child.

Betty was a little girl she was raising when Granny died.
To this day Betty still grieves over Valentine. Betty's
mother died in childbirth and Betty was only a few days
old when Granny took her in. Imagine that. A woman in
her eighties up all night with a little baby. Why, that'll
tear the hair out of a twenty-year-old, for heaven's sake.

I was working at a Safeway store when they called and
told me Grandma Valentine had died. Oh, that was a sad
day in Ballinger and all around for a couple hundred miles.
She had brought up so many kids just about everybody
was related to somebody she raised. Half the county was
at her funeral. It looked like the governor died or something. Just this plain ol' country woman and so many loved
her.

★

DEEP IN THE HEART OF TEXAS

Valentine was a real pioneer woman. Very strong. Very fair. A mind of her own. The kind of woman they built this country on. Now, she was a real Texas woman.

We were doing all right until my father died of spinal meningitis. Oh, he was the best-looking man. But a carbuncle came up on his neck. Of course, the ignorant doctors didn't help. They thought it was a boil. Why, he was dead in five days.

He was very young when he died and he left Mama with four babies. Mama never did seek other men though. She dedicated her life to her children. She always said, "Nobody but an idiot would look at me with four babies. And I don't need an idiot."

If there was ever a Southern lady, my mother was it. She'd always tell me, "Don't ever wear ragged underwear." And "Never answer the door with bare feet."

She instilled in me as a little tot that you can be proud of yourself regardless of whether you have any money or not. You're as good as anybody. You can do with your life whatever you want. Set your goals and struggle for it.

The only thing that bothered me was that Mama was very partial to my younger sister Sue. I was the oldest of four and I wasn't allowed to go out skating or join the other kids until all the chores were done. And that's not right.

The last thing that Mama told me before she died, she waved me over to her bed and called me by name,

"Katherine?"

"Yes, Mama."

"I want you to promise me something?"

"Anything, Mama."

"Will you promise to always take care of Sue?"

"You have my promise Mama. I will see to Sue."

★

I told Mama once, "You know, I could have hated you for favoring Sue." But I didn't. I loved her. I figured it wasn't Mama's fault. She was just partial to Sue. See, Sue was the good-looking one and the good-looking one is always pampered in a Southern family. Because the beautiful girl is highly valued.

Mama would introduce Sue by saying, "This is my pretty one." She'd slough me off. You can give a child a real complex if you slough 'em off like that. But I was the tough one and Mama knew that too. I guess I was a scrapper all my life. I came into the world afightin'. Nothing got me down.

After I lost my father I looked around and said, "There's a better way of life and I'm going to find it." I prayed to God every night to show me a way to help my mother.

The first job I got was in the sixth grade, just a child really, eleven or twelve. That was during the Depression and a woman took me in and trained me in the mercantile business. Ready-to-wear and general goods. That kind of thing. There was no pay. But she'd give me lingerie and material and things. That was very unusual back then because a lot of grown men didn't have jobs.

Oh, I was a go-getter. I worked after school, weekends, holidays. I stayed with her for six months and then J.C. Penny's offered me a job. For money. Daylight to midnight at Penny's and they paid me two dollars a day. In the seventh grade. Every dime, I gave to Mama.

When I married Joe he was a salesman for Ligget and Myers Tobacco. At that time it was considered a very good job, but they fired him and hired a college graduate for less money. People were desperate then. So Joe took a job in El Paso workin' for Safeway.

When we left Ballinger, we had a full tank of gas and fifty dollars. We landed in El Paso, paid the rent for a

★

week—that was forty-five dollars—then we had five dollars to live on before Joe got a paycheck. The apartment we moved into in El Paso was in the raunchiest part of town. I can't remember how many apartments shared the same bathroom but it was at least six. Every time I'd go down to take a bath, I'd take Lysol with me.

Nancy was just a few months old and the place didn't have a crib, of course. So, the first night, I rolled the divan up against the wall so Nancy couldn't roll off. I went down the next afternoon with Nancy to a furniture store and picked out the best youth bed that they had. And I said, "I have to have this delivered this afternoon for my baby."

"Certainly. How are you going to pay for it?"

"I'm going to charge it."

"Well, you'll have to talk to the credit manager."

"Okay."

I walked in, introduced myself, told them who I was and who Joe was with. Of course, we had no credit. And you know, that credit manager never said a thing to me. He just looked at me a long time and then said, "It'll be delivered this afternoon."

That's the way you did business in those days. You took a look at someone, sized up their character, and figured if they were good for it or not.

Joe and I lived on the wrong side of the tracks to save money. I told him, "We can't hurt Nancy livin' here because she's too young to know better. As long as we keep her in a good school, she'll be fine. Hold your head high. We have cheap rent. We're saving our money."

Joe thought I was crazy the way I'd save pennies and nickels. But as the pot started growing, he got excited too. He'd make a bonus, he'd put it in there.

After we put $10,000 away, I told him, "You're doing

★

well for Safeway. If you can do the same for us, we'll be doin' well too. Let's go into business for ourselves."

But, Joe was scared to death. They had brainwashed him, "You can't compete with Safeway. You can't compete with Safeway." And he kept throwing that in my face. I said, "The hell with Safeway. I know we can."

I finally nagged him into it and we opened a store in Roswell, New Mexico.

We worked hard, both of us. Three times a week I drove over to Portales, a hundred miles from Roswell, and bought eggs. See, Portales was egg country. Why, we made more money. I would buy eggs dirt cheap and drive around to the stores in Roswell and dicker on prices. I had an old truck that Liggett and Myers had in storage that we bought. No heat, no air conditioners and no windshield wipers. Slick tires. No insurance. I drove through every kind of weather in the world. I drove when it was snowin' so bad I couldn't keep it off my windshield. I'd hang my head out and I'd tie a scarf around my head and face and I'd drive down the center of the road so I could see where I was goin'. It was a hundred miles and one little filling station in between. Never did have any problem. If that old junker would have broke down I would have froze to death. Didn't even have a blanket in the car. See, youth has no fear—that's God's blessing.

After we'd been open five or six months and we were rolling along pretty good, Joe came home one evening with some news.

"Katherine, I've sold half interest in the store."

"You have?"

"Yes. I can get all our money out of it and still have half interest in it."

"There's only one thing wrong with that deal, Joe," I said.

★

DEEP IN THE HEART OF TEXAS

"What's that?"

"I have to sign the papers. And I won't do it. If we go down, we'll go down by ourselves."

We were doin' all right. But Joe was scared. Safeway had drilled it into him that you can't compete with the big boys. So even if we were doing good, he was shakin' all over.

But I always had confidence in myself. If you can do it, I can do it too.

I paid that store off in a year. Then we opened a second store and also bought a home. Paid cash for it.

Joe tried to sell out many times along the way but I wouldn't let him. Then we took another store and another store—goin' great guns. But do you know Joe was scared until the day we sold out, twenty-five years later, with eight stores and three a-buildin'.

Joe could have been a big-time operator. A really big-time operator. If he'd had any confidence. But he was a Mama's boy in the worst way. Joe had a domineering mother and that's why he was a namby-pamby. She ruined his life and she took a good shot at ruining mine. Except I wouldn't let her.

Joe's mother didn't like me from the start. But she never would have liked anybody that Joe married. She was from England. And she always threw it at us like a dirty wash-rag. She thought she was some damn aristocrat. Lady Cartlidge. Lady, my ass. I told Joe, "Hell, she was a peon over there." Now, Mr. Cartlidge had a nice background but he married beneath himself I figured. We never heard anything about her relatives. Where she came from. But she'd tell us constantly about Mr. Cartlidge. We were just Okies to her.

You talk about war. A mother-in-law can cause a lot of problems if a man isn't strong. See, Joe wouldn't stand up

★

to her. He was a Mama's boy. A six-foot-two-inch Mama's boy. I never could stand a titty-baby. Once childhood is over, cut the umbilical cord and get on with it.

When we got married, Joe and I just went to a little courthouse outside San Angelo. Didn't tell anyone. Just took a couple with us for witnessing. I don't even remember their names now.

Joe was still traveling for Ligget and Myers so he went right back out on the road that night and I went home to Mama and as soon as I walked in the door, I let her have it.

"Mama, I'm a married woman now."

She just bypassed that one. "Sure you are, sweetie."

"Okay, you're gonna get a license mailed to you."

Do you know he was scared to death to tell his mother we were married. Twenty-six years old! It was two months before I finally moved over to San Angelo with him. She had a fit when he finally told her.

When he lost his job with Ligget and Myers he stayed in San Angelo near his mother even though there weren't any jobs there. Finally, I had to tell him, "Either you leave San Angelo or I'm filing for divorce. We're gonna starve to death in San Angelo. There's nothing here for you. Get out!"

So he finally listened to me and he took the job in El Paso with Safeway.

His mother was jealous of anything that touched Joe. When we were in Roswell he was having a lot of trouble with his nerves. He went to one doctor after another. This one said an ulcer. This one, heart palpitations. That one said something else.

Finally, I told my doctor, "I'm having trouble with my husband. They've diagnosed him with so many things and we still haven't gotten to the bottom of it."

★

DEEP IN THE HEART OF TEXAS

So he said, "I'm going to make an appointment with another doctor I know."

Well, this doctor was a shrink, only we didn't know it until we got there. Joe passed out from heart palpitations when we got in his office. His nerves were just shot to pieces. And mine were too. All from that damn queen bee.

They took him immediately to the psychiatric wing of the hospital and checked him in. It was a great big beautiful place of a nuthouse. They had steel doors on that place to keep everyone in. But you know I made a lot of friends in that place. Probably belonged in there myself.

Anyway, I saw the doctor out in the hallway.

"What did you find wrong with him, doctor?"

"Your husband has the worst mother complex I have ever seen. That's all I'm going to tell you."

I had never mentioned mother to any doctor, let alone this one. But it only took him an hour to figure the whole thing out.

"I'm going to administer shock treatment."

I'm sure it was terrible at the time. They've improved on these things since then. They got one big Negro on one side and one on the other and two holding his shoulders.

When Joe came out of it, he didn't know his name or where he was. Nothing. It took two or three days for his mind to clear. They gave him five or six treatments. They'd wait three or four days and then they'd give him another one.

Joe begged me to get him out of there.

"No," I said, "you're gonna take another one. It isn't gonna kill you."

It did straighten out his mind about his mother though. He swore it didn't help him but it did. To the point where he could cope with her at least. She had the power to make

★

him feel bad if he didn't give in to her. And she demanded his constant attention.

Years later, after we sold out in Phoenix, we decided to move back to New Mexico and we had to ship her back with us. We had been hauling this miserable old woman around with us for all this length of time.

We had her set up in a rest home and she had broken her hip so she was in a wheelchair. I didn't know how we were gonna get her there. She wouldn't ride in an ambulance. So lo and behold, Joe makes her a bed in the back seat of my car. I knew right then I was in for the longest trip of my life. Phoenix to Roswell. Lord, that's a 700-mile trip. It's every bit of fourteen hours drivin'. And we were gonna do it in one day on account of her.

Anyway, we got her in the back and she had diapers on. I don't know what was the matter with her kidneys but they were just like her. They weren't any good either.

I had a new red Cadillac with white leather seats. So I had rubber sheets laid down in the back of the car. I told Joe, "She gets any wee-wee on my car, you've had it!"

Every few miles we'd have to stop and put her on a pot somewhere. Oh, Lord, it took Joe and I all we had to lift her out so she could go to the bathroom.

So anyway, Lady Cartlidge was in the back seat laying down and she couldn't sit up by herself, so she'd yell, "I want up! I want up!" Then, "Where's my son, Joe!"

"He's right in front of us."

So I'd pull up alongside of Joe and yell out the window, "Mama wants up!"

That's all we did all the way to Roswell, New Mexico. We'd pull her up and we'd start out again and we wouldn't go ten miles before she'd want down. Then she started screaming again that she wanted to go to the bathroom.

★

DEEP IN THE HEART OF TEXAS

So, finally, I had enough and I turned around and said, "Oh, just pee in your diapers, Lady Cartlidge."

Imagine all the people that would have liked to have said that to their mother-in-law?

By the end of the day I was nearly berserk. Up and down. All day long. I wanted to slap her to sleep.

Finally, we got to Las Cruces and we stopped and fed her. When I got back in the car, my nerves were like piano wire.

Now, when you come out of Alamogordo you start up into some mountains. It's a very windy, mountainous, two-lane road with a thousand-foot drop on both sides.

Well, I floorboarded it with her a-screechin' in the back. I turned up the radio all the way and I was singing to shut her out. Just a-bellowing at the top of my lungs.

I'd go around a corner full-throttle and she'd go banging around in the back, screaming the whole time. It's a wonder I didn't go off the cliff.

When I finally got to the rest home in Roswell I could hardly stand up, I was shaking so bad. When Joe pulled up, he went in the place and got an attendant and they took her inside.

I swore if I ever divorced Joe, the next husband would be a bastard and if he'd ever even heard of England, I'd have nothing to do with him. . . .

★

6

Mother was sitting under the hair dryer at Coiffure Continental when she heard Ron Chapman on KVIL announcing the upcoming Cowboys Cheerleaders tryouts.

"Alert all KVIL breathtakers. The Dallas Cowboys are holding their annual cheerleader tryouts next month. If you are 18 years of age and live or plan to move to the Metroplex area soon, send your application. . . ."

Mother leaned forward and got all the details of where to send the application. Then she sat back under the dryer. This was just what she'd been looking for. She figured Suzette, who was a 19-year-old sophomore at Texas Tech now, needed another challenge besides pageants and school since her pageant days were through.

We felt the odds were against us at 5ft. 5in. to enter Miss America or Miss U.S.A. pageants. We could take part in the Little Miss competitions because we weren't full-grown yet, and height wasn't an issue. But most of the girls who compete for Miss America are 5ft. 7in. and up. Why go into a situation where we knew we couldn't win? So Mother thought Cheerleader might be a good thing to try and a natural progression from our days as MacKenzie, Coronado, and Texas Tech cheerleaders.

She started planning.

The first thing to do, of course, was to get Suzette the right outfit—an outfit that would stand out in the crowd of

★

all those other girls, something that would be remembered. Mother spent the day shopping for fabric and finally stumbled on just the right thing: canary yellow material for shorts and a halter top. But there would need to be a purse and shoes to match. And the application said that each girl needed to have both high-heeled pumps and tennis shoes for the tryout performances. Mother found a canvas purse at Sanger Harris, and pumps at Neiman Marcus. Finding yellow tennis shoes to match the outfit however, was impossible.

Later, when Mother got back to Lubbock she went straight over to Dillard's and ordered a half-dozen pairs of size 6½M white tennis shoes and a case of Rit yellow dye. When everything arrived, we all sat around like we were coloring Easter eggs, trying to dye Suzette's shoes the perfect shade of yellow.

It's an old pageant trick. You go to the interviews in a yellow suit. Your costume is yellow. Your evening dress is yellow. Everyone remembers you just by the color. Of course, we weren't allowed to say our name in the tryouts. We were known only by our number. But Mother took care of that too. She had Suzette's name screaming at the judges—it was monogrammed across her handbag.

Mother sent Suzette to Sherry Allen over at Billy Jo's School of Dance in Lubbock. Sherry was young and up on the new jazz dancing that was the Cowboys Cheerleaders style. She put together a routine for Suzette that would showcase her talent. Even though the instructions accompanying the Cheerleader application said that contestants just had to do a little disco dancing for three minutes, Suzette showed up with a professionally choreographed routine.

When Mother and Daddy drove her to tryouts in Dallas in the spring of 1978, she was as ready as she'd ever be. In reality she had been preparing for that day all her life—dance lessons since she was three, beauty pageants since

★

she was six, cheerleader in junior high, high school, and at Texas Tech, and of course, daily attendance at Nancy Scholz's School of Charm.

The day of final tryouts, Sheri and I were in Lubbock literally glued to the phone. We would barely leave the front room. If one of us had to visit the little girl's room, the other one would move over within reach of the phone so she could grab it on the first ring.

We sweated through the entire day, getting madder and madder because no one had called us with at least an update. We didn't know that Mother and Daddy hadn't left the parking lot the whole day because Mother wouldn't let Daddy move that car an inch. "What if she comes out and we're gone?"

So the phone didn't ring until six that evening.

"Hello! Mother?"

"Stephanie, you're not going to believe this but your sister is now a Dallas Cowboys Cheerleader."

I started screaming and Sheri, even though she didn't have a clue what mother had said, started screaming too.

"Stephanie, there's a plane leaving Lubbock for Dallas in 45 minutes. Can you and Sheri make it?"

"You bet!"

Sheri and I filled four suitcases in five minutes and ran out the door. When we landed in Dallas, Mother and Daddy and Suzette picked us up and we drove off to Papillon's, an elegant restaurant, to celebrate. Then we went back to the Marriot off LBJ and fell asleep. The next morning is when the magic of the whole experience really hit us.

Mother and Daddy let us sleep in that morning. At around nine o'clock they came in to our adjoining room and dropped the morning papers on our beds. Splashed across the front page of both the *Dallas Times Herald* and the *Dallas Morning News* in full color was Suzette in her canary yellow outfit!

★

DEEP IN THE HEART OF TEXAS

The Dallas Cowboys were the new World Champions and the Dallas Cowboys Cheerleaders were America's Sweethearts back then. Suzette's photo was picked up by UPI and AP and appeared in papers all over America and the world. My sister was famous! It was like a fairy tale!

That was probably the greatest moment our family ever experienced. All of us were together there in the Marriot hotel and all of our dreams had come true.

The following year, the dream would come true for me too.

Ron Chapman, the KVIL superjock, was one of the judges for the Cheerleaders tryouts every year. That morning in April, 1979, when I tried out, Ron was motoring down the Stemmons, coming to grips with the day.

First off, Ron grumbled to himself good-naturedly, *it's eight in the damn morning. And, secondly, it's supposed to be my damn day off. And, thirdly, I have to stop by the KVIL studios on the way over and pick up the damn sound system . . . and Tex Schramm runs an organization worth 100 million dollars and he can't afford to buy a sound system for the Cheerleader tryouts? The Cowboys keep telling everyone how much of a loss it is to keep the Cheerleaders going. The Cheerleaders poster has been the biggest selling poster of all time, making that slinky number by Farrah Fawcett look like an army recruitment bill. The royalties off that alone could pay for twenty years' worth of tryouts and everything else the Cheerleaders did.*

Tex had the clout to get whatever he wanted from just about anybody in Texas since everybody wanted to be associated with the Cowboys. The team could afford anything they wanted, but why pay for it if somebody else would. Ron was the most popular d.j. in Dallas and had a lot of clout of his own. Yet here he was hauling over the sound system

★

with a big ol' smile on his face. And all those gorgeous girls were cheering for free.

"Ron, we don't have a sound system. Can you bring one from the station?"

"Sure. No problem."

Damn!

Just then a Corvette whooshed by, going about 80, and in it were two luscious blondes doing their makeup. The girl in the passenger seat was teasing her hair in the mirror of the sun visor and the driver was looking in the rearview using both hands to apply her eyeliner. Her eyes were locked on the mirror and her hands were busy with the fine details. Yet the car was tracking straight as a missile toward Texas Stadium.

In spite of his two-cuppa-coffee grouch, Ron smiled. Then he started chuckling. And then he remembered the real reason he kept doing this every year. Why, when someone said "Cheerleader tryouts," he got that uncontrollable warm inner glow. Then another car went by with another beauty. Then another and another. The closer he got to Texas Stadium the more he was surrounded in all lanes by gorgeous young females made up to please a prince.

He turned off the expressway and down the ramp, around the frontage road and into the Texas Stadium parking lot. In front of him was a sea of beauties—2,000 girls wearing shorts and halter tops with legs a hundred feet long. It was kind of like having a martini at eight A.M. It pinned his eyes back and woke his whole body up.

Two thousand fabulous females! he thought. *Nowhere else on earth had there ever been that many gorgeous girls all in one spot. A Vegas Show you might get 75 of them together. A beauty pageant maybe 50, 60 tops. A college campus might have four or five thousand women, but maybe a thousand are great looking and they're spread out all over campus.*

★

DEEP IN THE HEART OF TEXAS

They're not all enrolled in English IA at eight A.M. This was 2,000 gorgeous girls dressed in hot pants and high heels made up for a beach party.
Wow!

Besides all the beautiful women there were five judges and hundreds of photographers and cameramen. Every major station in Texas and the nation was there—CBS, ABC and NBC. Plus, writers and photographers from national magazines like *People*, *Redbook*, and *Life*. National coverage for some cheerleader tryouts? What was going on here?

Football is king in Texas because Texas is filled with macho men with nothing else to do. Friday night high school football is the only thing going in town. It's a social phenomenon. Moms, grandmas, grandpas, and all the kids come to the game.

The stars of the team are idolized and lionized all week. A guy throws five touchdowns and the principal declares it "Billy Don Wickers Day." On Friday afternoon the girls come out and lead cheers and chants to defeat the other team. The bonfire blazes and the coaches come up and give a little speech and even the minister shows up to throw in some hocus-pocus and a few prayers.

And then the incantations start.

"Who we gonna beat tonight?"

"The Cougars!"

"I can't hear you!"

"The Cougars!"

"Who?"

"THE COUGARS!"

You're ready to go kill somebody. All the time you snuggle up to your girl and pray for victory as the bonfire roars. It's a thrilling time that gives meaning to a small town life.

Football is a wonderful game, with the action and excite-

★

ment and the uniforms and all. But it would die overnight, abandoned like an old Chevy, if it weren't for the fans.

Take a kid dreaming about being a football hero. He's out in the backyard, football tucked under one arm, running. He jukes past the picnic table at the 35, hurdles the rainbird at midfield, cuts back, straight-arms the dog at the 30, cuts back again and he's in the clear, sailing to make the winning touchdown. And the whole time he can hear the crowd or maybe he's making those sound effects with his mouth like kids do, of 100,000 lunatics gone crazy, cheering their fool heads off for him.

Aaaahhhhhhhhhhhhhhhhhhhhhhhhhhhhhhhhhhhhhh!

Take that dream away and you kill football. Maybe it would still be played in the streets a little bit, but with no chance of making the cover of *Sports Illustrated* who would bother? And heroes . . . how are they made if there are no fans to cheer them on and carry them off the field? If there's no chance to neck with the head cheerleader in the back seat of Dad's Buick with the window fogging up, why bother with the game? In fact, it's the cheerleaders that really have a lot to do with making football what it is.

When you think of it the only difference between football and unloading a haytruck, of course, are those cheerleaders. A haybaler tackles those bales, gets bloody hands, an aching body, and has sweat pouring off him like a weeping willow after a rainstorm. The problem however, is that there's no one there to cheer all that effort. It's just hotter than hell, the pay stinks, and there's still half a skiff to unload.

Now, if haybalers could attract some cheerleaders, in a month they'd make an art form out of hauling hay. They'd be talking about this guy's powerful forearms and that guy's hand speed and there'd be nicknames and endorsement deals with glove companies and chewing tobacco and, of course, they'd be pushing beer.

★

DEEP IN THE HEART OF TEXAS

All that macho king of the hill, hero of the gridiron, and big deal businessman stuff is all just a game men play to attract a woman, specifically a beautiful woman. And from day one in Texas the beauties want to be the cheerleaders. That's the way it's always been. The little girls dream about growing up to be cheerleaders and the little boys want to grow up and do things to attract them . . . namely play football.

Nobody outside the state can quite understand just how big of a deal it is to be a cheerleader in Texas. Oh, it's an honor to be a cheerleader in Boise or Tallahassee or Kennebunkport all right, but in Texas it's nearly life or death. The dance studios are filled with seven-, eight-, and nine-year-old girls learning not ballet but drill team steps. If a child doesn't make a cheerleading squad in grade school, it's a family tragedy.

Sure, to the rest of the world the Dallas Cowboys Cheerleaders may be just a bunch of great-looking girls bouncing around on a football field on a weekend. But if you're from Texas and one day you get chosen to be a Cowboys Cheerleader, it's right up there with your wedding day. And depending on who you marry, it might even be bigger.

Some girls tried out two, three, four, and five times. And they kept on trying year after year. They took endless dance lessons and came to the tryouts with choreographed routines rehearsed for hours with elaborate costumes to match. You could tell by the quality of the girl that this was not just important but socially acceptable to boot.

The squad was made up of girls not only from Texas or from the United States, for that matter. Girls from all over the world tried out and were selected as Dallas Cowboys Cheerleaders. This elite group was the best that Texas had to offer and Texas was famous for its home-grown beauties.

Just about everything I did in life followed in my big sis-

★

ter's footsteps. Suzette had always led the way. She made cheerleader at MacKenzie Junior High, then Coronado High, and then Texas Tech. And so did I, because Suzette gave me the confidence I needed to do it. When she won the lead in the high school play, I auditioned the next year and I won it too.

I never felt I was in Suzette's shadow though because she was the best sister a girl could ever have. She was my best friend and liked by everybody. At just about every pageant she entered she was voted Miss Congeniality. Suzette is so upbeat, so friendly, so bubbly, and so helpful that right away a lot of people think she's phony. But there isn't a phony bone in her body. After people are around her for a while, they get caught up in her energy too.

When Suzette was retiring from the Cowboys Cheerleaders after four years with the team, Suzanne Mitchell brought her up in front of the whole team and said, "Suzette Scholz is the epitome of what a Dallas Cowboys Cheerleader is supposed to be." Suzanne handed out compliments about as often as a cow grows wings.

As soon as Suzette had been picked as a Cheerleader, I knew the next year I'd try out too. There I was with 2,000 other girls, but this wasn't the same as trying out for cheerleader at MacKenzie Junior High. This was the biggest moment of my life. This was everything a girl from Texas could ever dream about. I was trying out for the Dallas Cowboys Cheerleaders. And I was petrified.

That day, my parents dropped Suzette and me off at Texas Stadium and waited in the car for us while we went to tryouts. Suzette led me up a big ramp, then up a flight of escalators. As I rose higher and higher, first I saw the longest, tannest, fittest legs I'd ever seen, a whole room full of them. Then their bodies came into view; all were done up in tight shorts and halter tops with cleavage everywhere. Then

★

DEEP IN THE HEART OF TEXAS

I saw the hair and faces, and I wanted to turn right around and walk back down, but the escalator kept pushing us forward. *What am I doing here?* I said to myself. *I can't compete with these women. They're all so gorgeous.*

Everywhere I looked I saw cameras clicking and rolling, lighting up the place like a lineup. Sitting in the front row of all these girls, I recognized some of the most famous Cheerleaders, every one a celebrity in her own right.

There was *Julie Chambers*, the redhead with the sulky lips and sulky expression and sulky personality that drove men dippity-do. And *Nanette Atler*, the strawberry blonde with the pigtails and the freckled Norman Rockwell little girl face. And *Inger Jorgensen*, the breathtaking Swedish blonde, and *Ivonne Samuels*, the statuesque brunette with the green cats' eyes. And *Careene Miller*, the most famous Cheerleader of all, a Diana Ross look-alike that probably Diana herself wished she looked as good as. And next to Careene was my sister, Suzette.

While sitting in my chair, going over and over my routine in my head, I first saw *Bobby Sue Peck* with her mouth sort of half-open in awe and her eyes all glazed. It was obvious she didn't have a clue as to what she was doing here, just a country bumpkin with straight hair and tennis shoes.

The day before, she had been a student on a college campus tending to her own little world when a good friend stopped her.

"Hi, Bobby Sue."

"Well, hi," Bobby Sue said in that upbeat, top-of-the-morning way of hers. "How are you?"

"Just fine. There's a meeting tonight I think you should attend." And she handed Bobby Sue an ad that had appeared in the campus newspaper.

"Well, sure. Where is it?"

"*Houston Hall* at seven thirty."

★

"All right. I'll be there."

Bobby Sue was a cheerleader, she was in a sorority, and just about everything else on campus. She belonged to so many organizations she figured the meeting had something to do with one of them. So she made a mental note and stashed the ad in her purse.

That night when she showed up at Houston Hall, the sign above the door said, "Welcome to the Dallas Cowboys Cheerleaders sign-ups."

"Cowboys Cheerleaders? Is that what this is all about?"

"Yes, it is. I'm Suzanne Mitchell, the director of the Cheerleaders." Suzanne greeted her like she was a lost cousin and asked Bobby Sue to fill out an application. Then she invited her into a room for an interview.

"How do you like school, Bobby Sue? I see you've been very involved in activities here."

In college Bobby Sue had been selected as one of the "Most Beautiful" on campus. She had been photographed in a straw hat, a crop top, and jeans, holding a fishing pole for the cover of the school calendar. She looked like Debbie Reynolds in "Tammy and the Bachelor."

Suzanne needed a small town girl on the squad. A girl who could reach the common people. Somebody who could sign autographs and talk to some farmer or cowboy for thirty minutes about life in a small town.

After a few minutes of light conversation with Bobby Sue, Suzanne knew she had her girl.

And by the time she left the meeting Bobby Sue loved Suzanne. Suzanne had been warm and charming.

The next day Bobby Sue got a call. It was 7 A.M. and she was still in bed.

"Bobby Sue? This is Suzanne. I want you to show up tomorrow in Dallas for the semifinals of our tryouts."

"Tomorrow. I can't—"

★

"All the other girls have been through weeks of preliminary judging."

"But—"

"Wear high heels and shorts."

"I can't do that. My father would disown me."

"Okay, wear whatever you want. Just show up and let me handle everything. Congratulations!"

"Thanks . . ." Bobby Sue said, "but—"

Suzanne had already hung up.

So here she was at the Cheerleaders tryouts. In a daze, Bobby Sue wandered over to where the girls were all seated on folding chairs waiting for their turn to dance and interview with the judges. It was going to take all day so there was plenty of time to visit.

Bobby Sue sat down next to a voluptuous blonde.

"Hi, I'm Bobby Sue."

"Oh, hi, I'm *Pepper Patton*. What do you think?" And she sat up real straight with her shoulders pulled way back.

"About what?"

"About my boobs. Do you like them?"

"Fine, I guess."

"I just had them done for the tryouts."

"That's nice."

"Do you want to see them?"

"Well, I don't know."

"Come to the bathroom."

"Oh, I better not. I might miss my number when they call it."

"Oh, don't worry about that. I've been to three of these things. They won't get to us for hours. Come on."

So Bobby Sue and Pepper headed off for the bathroom, where Pepper lifted her T-shirt.

"What do you think? Aren't they nice?"

"Well, they sure are big!"

★

"Yeah, I know. I wanted them to be really impressive for the judges."

"Well, I sure am impressed."

When Bobby Sue got back to her chair, sitting next to her was a girl who was the spitting image of Jaqueline Smith on her favorite TV show, "Charlie's Angels."

"What's your name?"

"*Sandy*, but everybody calls me *Zee*."

"That's unusual."

"Short for New Zealand."

"Oh, of course, your accent."

Bobby Sue liked Zee right off. "You look 'em in the eye," Bobby Sue's daddy had always said. "And if they don't blush or blink, you can usually trust 'em." Zee, she soon found out, never blushed or blinked at anything. And she sure was interesting.

Right off they started talking about boyfriends.

"I've had the same boyfriend for six years now. Since I was 12. How about you?" asked Bobby Sue.

"I haven't had the same boyfriend for six minutes. Especially since I've been married."

"How long have you been married?"

"Oh, geez, it seems like years," Zee laughed. "But it's not on."

"It's not?"

"I mean we live together but I'm seeing the guy upstairs."

"Seeing?"

"It's just sex."

"Oh, I see," said Bobby Sue. But she didn't see at all. Bobby Sue was still a virgin and she could barely pronounce sex much less imagine it.

"146!" Suzanne called out.

"Oh, that's my number!" Zee said.

"Good luck!"

★

"Thanks!"

Kim watched while Zee did her routine. Kim had spent a whole year preparing for this. She'd dieted, taken dance classes, and run five miles every day like she was in training for the Olympics. This was her dream and she was going to give it all she had.

She had come to America with her parents from Taiwan when she was fifteen just about three years before. She went to her first high school pep rally a couple of weeks later and it changed her life. Everything was so loud and the people were screaming and yelling. It scared her to death. It looked to her like a bunch of cannibals getting ready for the feast.

But then the cheerleaders came dancing out on the stage and she fell in love.

"That's what I want to do," she thought to herself.

From that moment on, her ultimate goal was to be a Dallas Cowboys Cheerleader and now her chance had finally come. The only problem was that she was so petrified her legs wouldn't move. When Sandy was finished, Kim's number was called out. She stood up and walked slowly up to the stage and when her music started, she froze. She didn't know what to do. A whole year down the drain.

"Ni te piku!" (*Your ass!* in Mandarin) someone yelled out.

"Ni te piku?" Kim thought and looked around and there was *Lisa* grinning that devilish grin of hers. Kim just couldn't help herself and broke up laughing. Then she regathered her composure and knew she was going to be all right. When they started the music over for her, she flew into her routine.

Thank god for crazy Lisa. She'd seen this poor girl from Taiwan up there about ready to fold and she yelled out the only Oriental cuss words she'd learned on last year's USO tour. From that moment on, the shy Taiwanese girl and the rebel were best friends.

★

Lisa was last up. This was fine with all the other girls because Lisa was the show stopper and nobody wanted to follow her anyway. Texie Waterman, the Cheerleaders' choreographer, smiled. She always smiled around Lisa, who was the best dancer the Cheerleaders ever had or were ever likely to have. She could do anything. She could dance, sing, act . . . anything. Everybody else was average compared to Lisa. She'd do a jump and spread-eagle her legs at least ten feet off the ground. And Texie would just smile with that cigarette she always had, dangling from the tips of her fingers.

Lisa and Texie were cut from the same cloth. They were both gypsies who set their own ground rules, free spirits who pursued eccentricity as a mark of excellence. But Texie and Lisa could pull it off because they had something in common—talent.

Lisa wanted to be a dancer and a star, to travel to Broadway and Hollywood. That's what Texie had done. Texie was born in Dallas but took off for New York when she was 18 to study with Peter Gennaro and Nico Charisse, among others. Within a year she was on Broadway, appearing in the original Broadway cast of "My Fair Lady" and working with Imogene Coca in "Wonderful Town." She met and married her first husband, Arte Johnson of *Laugh-in* fame. Texie was also hired by Sid Caesar to dance on his show. She had done it all. When she wasn't working in New York, she traveled the country doing musicals, nightclub revues, and summer stock.

No matter what Tex Schramm's P.R. machine pumped out about it being his and Suzanne Mitchell's idea to have showgirls on the football field, it was really Texie who was a major part of the genius behind the Cowboys Cheerleaders. It's hard to imagine a desk-bound executive being the genius

★

behind a dance troupe like the Cheerleaders. Everyone believed it though. Schramm always knew that if he told the public something loud enough and long enough, they'd buy it.

Texie Waterman was one of a kind. She was a great jazz dancer in her own right and a great choreographer. She had a unique style—the Texie Waterman style. Like any choreographer out there, from Martha Graham to Paula Abdul, a Texie Waterman dance had a style of its own. There was just something about it; her signature was distinct.

It was Texie Waterman and her style that set the Dallas Cowboys Cheerleaders apart. She was the author of the New York style of jazz dancing that exploded onto the field with a sassy, "look out" exuberance. The Cheerleaders were Texas today. Everything was big—big steps, big movements, big kicks. Everything was exaggerated to fit their mammoth stage.

Texie Waterman created sports entertainment dancing. No one before had ever heard of a dancing squad for a sports team. She pioneered a new form—what it looked like and how people reacted to it. Everybody else followed in her footsteps—even Paula Abdul owes a debt to Texie. The Laker Girls are the progeny of the Cowboys Cheerleaders. These two have been the only unique sports entertainment groups. Everybody else was just an imitation.

After Lisa's dance routine, the judges got busy tallying their votes. But there was a problem.

Ron Chapman and Suzanne butted heads from the beginning over *Starr*, one of the tryout candidates.

"What's wrong with her?" Ron wanted to know.

"We don't care for her kind."

"Okay, let me get this straight. Gorgeous and talented is out."

★

"It's her attitude."

"Her attitude?"

"She's ambitious."

"Everybody in this room is ambitious. I'm ambitious. You're ambitious."

"We don't want the kind of girl who wants to use the Cheerleaders as a stepping stone to a movie or singing or modeling career."

"What do you want them to use it for? A stepping stone to the secretarial pool?"

"It's not a stepping stone at all. It's a privilege that a few lucky girls get the good fortune of experiencing for a year."

"Yeah, I know the party line. But how about the fans?"

"I'm thinking of the fans. The fans want a girl they can relate to. The All-American girl next door."

"How many girls living next door to you have bodies like *that* stuffed into hot pants and a halter top?"

"That's the show business part of it, Ron."

"That's my point. The greatest show on earth to the fans is the greatest looking girls we can find. They want girls who look great in their binoculars."

"She's out, Ron."

"She's in, Suzanne. Or I'm out."

Starr's sin was that her singing was openly seductive. When she sang, she sang right to the male judges. And she could really sing.

"Cry me a riveeeeeer. Crrrrrrry me a ri-ver. Ohhhhhh, I cried a river over you." And she sang it right into Ron's eyes and his heart.

Starr just had that Southern charm oozing out of her and she knew how to apply large amounts of that sweet honey on a man. To Starr it was all a game. She knew how to turn

★

a man on. And Suzanne had trouble with her from the minute her beautiful face flashed that knock-em-dead smile.

Ron and Suzanne had fought over a lot of girls before. If Suzanne took a disliking to her, the girl could have danced on the moon after that and it wouldn't matter. It didn't make any difference what Ron said. She was out.

But not this time! If he didn't get Starr, he was going to walk out and he was taking his "goddamn sound system" with him!

Ron liked to pretend he really didn't care about these tryouts, that it was all just a lark; pick a bunch of girls out for a cheerleading squad . . . just a job. Yes, it had its moments, but why should he care if one girl got picked and another didn't. At least that's what he told himself. But the truth was he really did care. He believed in the same illusions that these girls believed in. After all, it was he who helped create the All-American, girl-next-door image of the Cheerleaders by masterminding all the hype on KVIL. But he believed . . . Damn it! These girls weren't Suzanne Mitchell's private harem, no matter what she might think. They belonged to the fans—to Dallas, to Texas, and yes, they belonged to America. It was all a part of Tex Schramm's media snowjob but still it was true. They *were* America's Sweethearts. They *were* the 36 most beautiful girls in Texas.

So Ron fought. "Hey, I didn't get up at 6:30 in the morning to be blown away just at your whim. This girl is a knockout! I want her or you can judge this thing without me."

Suzanne pinned him with her steely, all business look. "Okay Ron. If you feel that strongly about it, she's yours."

The final squad of 36 was announced the next morning. The judges met and debated through the night to come up with final selections. It was difficult to narrow down the bevy of beauties because there were so many talented and intel-

★

ligent women to choose from. Of course it was hardest on the girls. They sat or walked around, nervously chattering while they chewed on their seventy-five-dollar acrylics.

Finally, Ron Chapman came to the microphone and the whole place quieted down on cue.

"Ladies, the judges have come to their decision. When your number is called, please come up front and stand next to me. These numbers are in no particular order. So without further ado here are the 1979 Dallas Cowboys Cheerleaders. Number 64, Number 12 . . ."

He started rattling off numbers and before the first fifteen were called, Suzette had made it and Bobby Sue and Sandy and Kim and of course, Lisa. When he had called out twenty numbers, I gathered up all my stuff in my bags. I was ready to leave and already trying to think up what I was going to tell my parents.

They continued calling out numbers, my heart pounding faster and faster as they announced. When they were about two-thirds of the way through I started to panic. I began counting the number of girls already on the stage—22, 23, 24, 25, 26 . . .

When they got to the 30s my heart was sinking like a Texas sunset—31, 32, 33 . . . oh, no, this is it. . . . What am I going to tell my poor mother and father sitting out there in the car? . . . Oh well, Suzette will still be a Cheerleader at least. . . . 34, 35 . . .

"And the last girl to be selected is Number 57."

That was my number! But I still couldn't believe it. It wasn't until I heard Suzette up on the stage scream, "Stephanie!" that it really hit me. That's when I knew I was a Cheerleader.

The entire place was bedlam. Girls were running all over hugging and kissing each other; and crying, everyone was

★

crying. The photographers, five and six deep, snapped away at the spectacle.

In the midst of all the chaos I battled my way up front. Somehow Suzette found me and we just stood there hugging each other and crying. Not too many dreams come true in life. But this was one of them. I was a Dallas Cowboys Cheerleader!

Barbara Burns was another girl that made the team that day. She was a brunette who looked like Dorothy Hamill, complete with the same haircut and the same sparkling eyes. While driving home after tryouts she had to pull over just to cry for a while.

At home, Barbara's mother, sister, and best friend were all waiting for her. Their house was across the street from a big park and on weekends the place was packed with men playing ball. Picture the scene.

Barbara pulls up and gets out of her car all decked out in hot pants and high heels. Then three women come screaming out the front door.

The timing was perfect. Barbara's sister would wash her hair every Sunday morning, put it up in a towel, put on a wraparound terrycloth robe, and do her nails. Barbara had pulled up right in the middle of the whole ritual and her sister came running out with wet nails, trying to hold her terrycloth wraparound with her elbows.

Across the street finishing off their after-game drinks was this huge group of men. What do you suppose they were thinking? First they see what looks like a hooker drive up, then an old lady comes screaming out of the house, and behind her is a half-naked girl trying to hold up her towel while trying not to ruin her nails. Thinking? . . . Nothing! They all stood there, jumping up and down, screaming out their reaction.

★

Poor *Sadie Staakt* however, was another story. She didn't make the squad, but *Playboy* spotted her and a couple of months later she was Playmate of the month. In her layout was a shot of her at the Cheerleaders tryouts, sitting in the middle of a group of contestants, several of them looking very bewildered.

★

O ne of the first things we did together as a squad was go on a big campout. We all met at Texie's studio and drove caravan style to a big ranch out past Lake Dallas. As soon as we got there I knew I was in for a long day and night.

Everybody was dressed in cutoff jeans and tennis shoes, but I had on hot pink leather shorts, hot pink high heels, a silk blouse, and a leather cowboy hat. I looked sensational! Suzette had kept telling me to wear something for camping. But if you've never been camping, how are you supposed to know what to wear? The only other girl dressed like me was Careene Miller. She stepped out of the van in tight-fitting blue-jeans stuffed into her red sueded high-heeled boots. Careene looked fabulous! I'm sure she'll go to her grave in a mink.

This was going to be a real experience. I was looking forward to sleeping under the stars, but I had no idea that there would be so many bugs in the wilderness. My skin began to crawl just thinking about which bedbug might be joining me in my sleeping bag. Thank God for Careene.

Careene was by far the funniest Cowboys Cheerleader and her sense of humor was completely uninhibited. Her figure was also unique. She had enormous breasts but from there on down was less and less of her. Her legs were nothing but little ol' broomsticks. The white boots that most of us strained to zip over our calves fit her like galoshes.

★

Nothing could keep Careene down. She was in the hospital one year with a kidney infection that had her confined to her bed. At least that's what the doctors thought.

"I'm very sorry," they told her, "but you need to be on an I.V., so there's no way you can leave and go to tryouts. You'll never get over this infection if you don't stay in bed."

Every year we had to try out all over again even if we had been on the team for a decade. It didn't matter. If we missed tryouts we could not make the team. Suzanne Mitchell accepted no excuses. The fact that Careene had cheered her guts out for eight years meant nothing.

Well, the doctors never calculated just how much Careene wanted to continue on as a Cowboys Cheerleader. That night she was out in the hallway with the I.V. pole in one hand and the glucose bottle in the other, practicing her high kicks and splits. The next day she unhooked herself from the tubes, drove to tryouts, and danced her way onto the team.

As soon as Careene spotted me at the campout, she came running over.

"Stephanie! Girl, I'm soooo glad I've found somebody else who's civilized! I've been coming to these horrible expeditions for six years now. You stick with me!"

Careene had a can of "Raid" in one hand and a can of "OFF!" bug repellent in the other. She'd give a little psssssst of one when she wanted to emphasize a point.

"What do you think they're doing dragging us out here? I mean they built *Dallas* didn't they, to get away from all this?"

Pssssst! Psssssst!

"And there isn't a man for a thousand miles!" Careene strutted around the campfire in her usual irreverent routine, describing in sarcastic terms the symbiotic relationship the Cheerleaders shared with the high rollers of "Big D."

"It's just like the old cliche," she cooed, as we all giggled

★

in response. "You can't live with 'em and you can't live without 'em. And that goes for the rich ones too! Where are they hidin' all the men around here? Whatever am I going to do out here all alone? I feel simply naked without a bunch of men around. Y'know what I mean?"

We played a lot of camp games that afternoon; just a bunch of girls alone together. And Careene, despite her speech, had the most fun. But then Careene always did.

I had never had that much fun with other women before and I never really knew why. But this was a special group. There were no jealousies, and that was something none of us had ever encountered before.

We were all the same type—intelligent, talented, vivacious women ready to take on the world. Almost every girl had been Homecoming Queen, Varsity cheerleader, the lead in the school play, Valedictorian, Honor Roll, "Most Beautiful," "Mostly Likely to Succeed," and so on. A bunch of overachievers, and suddenly for the first time we were with a group of our peers.

When I was young, I didn't understand jealousy. I found a little place to call my own; my world of make-believe was very real to me. I would dance alone in the backyard, or in front of the mirror. And I would spend hours down in our basement creating screenplays, puppet shows, or fashion designs for my dolls. Although I enjoyed being by myself, I loved being popular and winning Valentine Sweetheart, Class Favorite, and Head Cheerleader. Then I discovered that sometimes being popular is just another form of solitude.

But with the girls on the squad it was different. There was no back-stabbing or envy. We had all received honors while growing up. The Dallas Cowboys Cheerleaders were the crème de la crème, the Class of the League. We were with our own, and it felt comfortable.

★

That day there was a bonding between us. We played together, sunbathed, swam, and then we had a big Texas cookout and ate till we busted. It was the last real meal most of us would have for a long time.

When the sun started going down, Suzanne took us out in the middle of this big ol' pasture in the middle of Texas. We built a big fire and there was nothing but us and our sleeping bags and those big Texas stars.

When the fire got roaring, Suzanne quieted us down.

"You girls have been chosen to be a part of a very elite group. The best of the best. There are millions of girls all over America that would like to be in your place right now. Don't ever forget that.

"I want you to take the next few hours to get to know each other. You are going to be spending a lot of time together in the next year. There are going to be good times and bad times. You're going to laugh together and cry together. And you've got to learn to pull together.

"I want each girl to stand up and tell us something about yourself. Share something personal. Maybe some little secret."

I don't know what it was but as soon as those logs got roaring, we just let down our hair and all those personal, revealing stories about our lives came tumbling out and suddenly, we weren't strangers anymore. The mood really started building and some girls stood up for an hour and poured their hearts out. It was like doing a little striptease. Everybody got into it like going skinny-dipping.

"Bobby Sue, why don't you start?"

"Me?"

"Sure, go ahead."

"Well, I can tell you what my most embarrassing moment was. It happened when I was nine years old. We were all eating Mexican food at my house one night and all this com-

★

pany was over. I was wearing these pants made of really thin cotton that my mother had made. So my parents and friends were playing cards, sitting around the table, and I was standing there looking at their cards and something slipped and I broke wind and blew the seat of my pants right out."

"Nooooo."

"Yes! Only the worst part of it was I didn't know it. They were all laughing at me and I thought it was because of my 'toot' and the whole time it was because I'd blown this big ol' hole in my seat."

We all laughed for a while. Then Kim got up.

"The first day I went to school in America I thought I was watching an X-rated movie. That's how different the Taiwanese culture is. Holding hands is a big step in Taiwan.

"The most sex I'd ever seen was when I went to see "The Sound of Music" and the young boy kissed the young girl in the summer house. That was going all the way to me. So when I walked into school that first day and all the kids were kissing and petting, I thought I was watching *Deep Throat*.

"I won the Miss Taiwan/USA Contest last year and I flew back to Taiwan to compete for Miss Taiwan. After being in the United States for three years I found Taiwan weird. Girls go around holding hands with other girls and boys link arms with boys.

"I didn't say anything to my Taiwanese friends but inside I was very uncomfortable. That's when I knew I had become very Americanized in a short time. Before I went back, I thought I was a Taiwanese girl in America. Then I wondered if maybe I was an American girl who had been born in Taiwan."

"Okay, Zee, it's your turn."

Zee looked around at all of us for a little while. Then she

★

plunged right in. She had already had more adventures than all of us put together.

"My parents were pioneer types. The kind who would have signed up for the Oregon Trail. Dad was a self-styled missionary. He had a vision one night that he was meant to teach the Aborigines a little religion. So when I was 18 months old, they borrowed forty dollars from my grandparents and took off from New Zealand for the Australian Outback out near Alice Springs to convert the Aborigines. Alice Springs is in the middle of nowhere. All that's there are a bunch of black people and a big rock. So I grew up wondering why I was white because everybody around me was black.

"From Alice Springs we went to Melville Island off the coast of Darwin. We were a canoe ride away from New Guinea where headhunters still plied their trade. Then we packed up again and moved into the mountains of Sri Lanka, 6000 feet up. My parents taught the natives, while in the cities below there was a revolution going on. We had to evacuate the village a couple of times when the guerrillas showed up. Never bothered my parents a bit.

"It seems pretty exciting when you hear how I grew up but I felt I was in prison with this religion of my parents. I didn't believe it. I didn't follow it. I was forced into it. When I was 16, a Catholic school friend and I went flying with her local priest. He was a private pilot. I skipped church to go, and I became a sort of an outcast. But the funny thing is I had every guy in the church chasing me from then on.

"The first chance I had to get out of there, I grabbed it. When I turned 18 I received insurance money from a terrible automobile accident I had suffered. So I took the money and came to America.

"See, when I was 12, I was in a head-on collision at 50 mph coming back from church. My parents were in the car

★

behind me. I flew up and hit my forehead and nose on the courtesy light on the ceiling of the car, came back down, and broke my jaw on the back of the front seat. My forehead was pushed back into my cerebral cortex.

"I had a five-hour operation to put my forehead back together again and reconstruct the bridge of my nose, which was flattened. They spent much of the time picking bone chips out of my cerebral fluid. Periodically, pieces of bone come out of my forehead through the skin.

"I was in the hospital for three weeks. My teeth were wired together for eight weeks. One night my nose started bleeding and I almost choked to death on my own blood.

"I had extensive dental work to cap the broken front teeth but I looked pretty bad from the time I was 12 until I was 18. And, of course, the kids in school taunted me. Called me scarface. For years that was my name. Not Sandy or Zee . . . Scarface.

"So now when I look in the mirror I don't see a pretty girl, I see scars. People tell me all the time I'm beautiful. But it's like someone describing music to a deaf person. All I see are the scars."

We were all quiet for a while after that. Zee was crying softly and Bobby Sue put her hand gently around her shoulders. To try and liven things up a little, Starr got up and made up some one-liners for relief.

"I learned to make love from a preacher boy. Preacher's sons are the worst. Well, the worst or the best. It depends on how you look at it."

"I hear you, sister," *Chantelle Roosevelt* called out, like she was at a Baptist revival.

"Well, I must have thought he was the best," Starr said, "because I wanted to get married in the worst way. I was only seventeen. I had a terrible fascination with the guy. Dark hair, dark eyes. God, was I head-over-heels."

★

"I know what you're sayin', girl."

"I had to chase that man down. Oh, it was very frustrating. Took me nearly three weeks!"

"A woman's got to have what a woman's got to have, honey!"

"Turned out to be an animal though."

"Oh, they're all alike!"

Starr and Chantelle went on that way for ten minutes until that boy didn't stand a prayer. By the time they were through, we were all rolling around on the ground laughing hysterically.

It was getting late by then and the stars were straight overhead, as bright as diamonds. Despite Starr and Chantelle, things turned very serious. Girls started telling about their alcoholic parents. One girl had been tossed around from foster home to foster home. They just poured their hearts out.

Barbara Burns got up next.

"My father divorced my mother when I was eight. I was a latch-key kid and I remember walking home from school and pretending that when I opened the door my mother would be home baking cookies. I always wanted her to be there and she never was because she had to go out and work and support three little children. All my life I pretended to have babies and play house. If someone would ask me what I wanted to be when I grew up, I'd always answer, 'I want to have kids and make a home for them.' "

After Barbara, most of the girls who got up were already crying—already coming apart, spilling out all over, pouring themselves into our hearts and beyond into the dark, soulless sky.

Suzanne sat quietly in the darkness beyond the firelight and let us talk. Then, it was Lisa's turn.

She sat there a very long time before she spoke. Most of

★

us knew what was eating at the core of her soul. Lisa's father was the vice president of a bank. He had flown down to Florida in the corporate jet six months before for a groundbreaking. On the way back, the plane went down and everyone was killed. And in Lisa's life, that touched off a spiritual hurricane that she was still reeling from. Lisa was hanging on as tight as she could but her life was blowing apart and she didn't know how to stop it.

"Ever since my father died," she started slowly, "I can't really sleep at night because I'm afraid of the dark. I'd never been afraid of the dark even when I was a little girl. But now I'm afraid."

Lisa lay down in the dirt with her face tucked into her elbow and cried like I'd never heard anyone cry.

"I hate God for taking my father away from me. I can't help it. I loved him so much."

Kim went over and took Lisa in her arms and rocked her gently and cried with her. We were all crying and hugging each other, hugging Lisa and Kim and crying. Crying for each other and ourselves. Crying because we'd finally found friends that we could love. Crying because we were just a bunch of pleasers who'd been trying to please all our lives.

It wasn't any accident that we were all together. Suzanne had handpicked us all. Sure, we could all dance and we looked great but so did most of the other 2,000 girls who tried out. Suzanne picked us because she knew we were all going to wrench our guts out to get her approval, to please her anyway she wanted.

That's what Ron didn't understand when he fought for Starr. Suzanne knew Starr wasn't what she was looking for. Starr didn't need to cut her wrists and bleed all over herself.

★

hen my sisters and I were all selected to be Dallas
Cowboys Cheerleaders, we stepped aboard a
rocket ship that was about to be launched to the
moon.

In the late seventies and early eighties, Texas—
Dallas in particular—was riding the crest of an enormous
financial boom. There were high rollers everywhere. Oil was
gushing out of the ground at more than forty dollars a barrel
and up. Land prices were spiraling upwards at a dizzying
pace.

Texas was the prime beneficiary of the panic that hit
America when the Arabs cut off our oil supply. Overnight,
oil quadrupled in price. While the rest of the country plummeted into recession in the mid seventies, Dallas, the financial center for all those oil fields, boomed.

Fueled by all that oil money, land prices skyrocketed. All
anyone had to do in Texas was buy an apartment complex,
fix it up, raise the rent, and sell it a year or two later for
twice the original price. Everybody was a financial genius!

Dallas grew like mesquite on the prairie. The state bird
was the building crane. You'd leave town for a month and
two more skyscrapers would be there when you got back.
A significant portion of today's Dallas skyline was built in
just three or four years.

It was a high-rolling, hysterical time. You know those
stories about the Arab sheiks with their 747s, their mansions

★

in Beverly Hills, and those shopping trips at Harrod's when they closed up the store so the sheiks could shop all alone and spend a million or two in a day? Well, the oil money was also pouring into Texas and the same kind of extravagant excess was running wild in Dallas. And then in the eighties, Texans discovered a new kind of gusher; one that was clearer, easier, and quicker than Spindletop. It was known as the Savings and Loan Association.

Silver Clouds were okay but a Bentley meant the owner had gone out there and really searched for the most conspicuous extravagance. A Bentley was a head-snapper. Or a Lamborghini or an Excalibur. Those fit the bill too. Even the maid drove a Mercedes to the store.

The city was hopping. People went out on Monday or Tuesday night as if they were weekend nights. The cafes were overflowing. The night clubs never had an off night. Forget the weekends. Only people who knew somebody could find a table at a decent restaurant or get into any of the hot clubs. Dallas was on full throttle seven days a week.

The social center of Dallas, and all the Southwest for that matter, was Texas Stadium. That's where all the big spenders, all the power brokers met.

American football was born in the Ivy League schools back east but when it made its way down to Texas, it was turned into something akin to war. Football was a simple game in which a player pitted himself against the brawn and wit and speed of his enemy. Texans like that kind of uncomplicated brutality. A Texan, even if he's a scrawny accountant, thinks of himself as rugged, like it was him with John Wayne at the Alamo. Once he had fought that battle like a man, he could go back to balancing the books at Ernst and Whinney.

The cult of football, money, and power all came together under that glittering blue and silver dome—that pantheon to conspicuous spending and the gaudy Texas myth which

★

the TV ratings of "Dallas" were built on. J.R. was not a fictional character! There were hundreds of them at Texas Stadium every Sunday.

The private airports around Dallas couldn't accommodate all the private jets that flew into the city on Sunday for the game. There was a mile-long line of limos that serpentined through the parking lot out Gate 8 (for limos only) and down the highway leading up to the stadium. They pulled up one after another and dropped off their big-deal passengers.

It would be 95, sometimes 100 degrees out and the women would come sashaying into the stadium in sables and leathers. Jewels dripped off every appendage that would hold a bauble, and diamonds were everywhere—in their ears, around their neck, around their wrist and ankle, and draped in their hair or around their waist on a belt. You couldn't tell if their watch told time; it had so many diamonds on the face and solid diamonds studding the band.

The entire Who's Who of the Southwest have owned a suite at Texas Stadium at one time or another. It's something that has to be done like showing up at the Cattle Baron's Ball or eating lunch at The Mansion on Turtle Creek. The game is a social event. Edwin L. Cox, former mayor Starke Taylor, Danny L. Faulkner, Trammel Crow, Lawrence R. Herkimer who founded the National Cheerleading Association and invented the Herky Jump—they've all had suites. And so have corporations like Dr. Pepper/7-Up and American Airlines and Mary Kay Cosmetics. And of course, Daddy had to have a suite too, right next to the KVIL FM-AM Infinity Broadcasting suite.

Some of the suites were going for a million and up. And that's just the bare walls. Then the owner would dump another million in it trying to make it look like a combination of Versailles and Caesar's Palace.

Our suite was of particular interest because by the time

★

DEEP IN THE HEART OF TEXAS

Sheri became a Cheerleader, Mother had all three of our pictures prominently displayed on the wall. There had never been three sisters on the squad in the history of the Dallas Cowboys Cheerleaders and my parents were very proud of us.

Normally, suites had ten seats overlooking the field and then a bar area behind that. Some people even bought two suites and knocked the walls out. Oh, they were something. Many had computers with up-to-date stats on all the players. A fan could punch up Tony Dorsett and find out how many yards he'd gained so far that season. Some suites had five satellite dishes wired up to them so it was possible to watch any football game going on in the country.

So, for a one or two mil' investment (plus catering and entertainment expenses), a fan who owned a suite could come to Texas Stadium for maybe eleven games a year. That's three hundred square feet of space for 40 or 50 hours a year. People with money were crawling all over each other to get in line for the privilege of owning one. The real kicker was that if you owned one of these million dollar suites you still had to buy a ticket to get in the game.

There were a lot of people in these suites that never even saw the game. People would be walking from one suite to another socializing. The women were all dressed up and most didn't give a damn about the game anyway. They were gabbing about who was divorcing whom, who had gained weight, who was wearing what, and who looked like hell at the Crystal Charity Ball while they sipped their frog water or the "pooey foosey."

If anyone started cheering, they'd look up from their gossip and say, "What happened?"

"Dorsett's running for a TD."

"Oh, go Tony, go. That guy can run, can't he."

Those big-rich Texans sat up in their suites like royalty.

★

And why wouldn't they think they'd inherited the kingdom? They had all the money in the world, and their football team, which was their religion, never lost. Once in a while the Cowboys would get behind, but then Staubach would start another miracle at just about the time the whiskey and Dom Perignon was kicking in. St. Roger would kneel in the huddle and the whole stadium would say a little prayer. . . . *Two minutes to play. Pass to Drew Pearson, swing to Dorsett. Bang, bang, bang, down the field. Nothing to worry about. Have another Jack Daniels. Just starting to feel good*—the alcohol and Staubach's magic crescendoing in the brain. All that money like a symphony playing background to every move. And every move is right. You're a genius. Staubach's a genius. *Twenty seconds left. Over the middle to Tony Hill! Touchdown! Yeeeeeeeeeeeeessssssssss! Allllll Right!* Scream and yell for a few minutes, slap a bunch of buddies on the back. High fives. Low fives. Knock back the rest of that drink and head on down the hall to the Stadium Club.

After the game, everybody from the suites would adjourn to the Club. When the gun sounded, the band would strike the first note and in no time at all the high rollers were in there dancing and drinking and eating and celebrating another victory, another affirmation that being a Texan was the best goddamn thing to be in this whole goddamn world.

That's where I got to know Ed McBirney. After the game I would get dressed and join my father and mother up in the Club. One night I walked in wearing a pair of skin tight black leather pants and when Ed saw me, his eyes fell out of his head and rolled around on the floor for a while.

My father motioned me over. "I want you to meet Ed McBirney."

"Hi, Ed! I've met you before, when I was very, very young. It was at the Hilton Hotel on Mockingbird. I must

★

have been all of thirteen with braids and braces on my teeth."

"Well, you're all grown up now, aren't you," he said. Then he leaned over to my father.

"When can I marry your daughter, Ken?"

"Ed, you son of a bitch, you'll never be good enough for my daughter." They both laughed like it was a big joke. But it wasn't any joke to Daddy. He knew what kind of man McBirney was. He devoted a good deal of his time to spending money, but back then he was a god in this town. He was riding high in Dallas and everybody loved him.

Don Dixon and "Fast Eddie" McBirney: A couple of the biggest swindlers currently facing possible jail time for the S&L failures that may take this country 30 years to recover from. Dixon's the bandit who took all our money and spent it on yachts and whores. Back then those guys were heroes. They were Horatio Alger in spurs. They were the myth and legend of the Texas wildcatter who hits the gusher; the guy driving the Cadillac with a pair of long horns bolted to the hood and a pinkie ring the size of Rhode Island. They were the American Dream come true.

Just a few years before, another Texas millionaire had been a house painter. He had even painted the suites at Texas Stadium. A few years later he was flying in on his Lear 55 and he owned one of those suites. He liked to take you around and show you the job he did on Ross Perot's place.

"Fast Eddie" was like a Good Humor Man peddling Eskimo Pies out of a truck when he slick-talked his way into a big real estate transaction. In a state where wheeler-dealers were as common as Rolex watches, "Fast Eddie" quickly proved to be one of the biggest of them all. He was the quintessential Big Dealer—fast movin', hard drivin'.

Ed was a smooth operator who could have sold fur coats in hell. He was the kind of "Big D" wildcatter who would be

★

comfortable sipping Dom Perignon and Chateau Lafitte Rothschild over a client lunch. Sunbelt sultans didn't blink an eye when it came to running up $50,000 entertainment tabs at The Mansion on Turtle Creek. Anything for a sale or a good time.

That's how you hustle people in Texas. You want some bigshot to buy a ten million dollar building, you've got to entertain him. Pick him up in your Gulfstream, bring him into town, and talk about four or five different properties at a time while you're sitting behind your Koa wood desk.

"Hey, got it done. Let's go eat!" Take him to the best restaurant. Pick up a couple of beauties on the way if the wife isn't along. It's all part of deal making.

A few days after we met at the Stadium Club, Ed called, "Stephanie? This is Ed McBirney. I'd like to take you out."

"What did you have in mind?"

"Thought we'd go to Hawaii," he laughed.

"My daddy has the biggest shotgun you ever saw, Ed."

"Yeah, and he's mean too. How about dinner? See you at six."

Ed wasn't bad looking, tall and lanky, dark hair and dark eyes, and obscenely rich. It sounded like fun.

At the time, Ed was in his heyday. He was in the paper about every other day for some big land deal he'd managed. The way he tossed money around was legendary. He threw parties at the sound stage over at Las Colinas that cost hundreds of thousands of dollars, like the "African Safari" we went to. McBirney had them build an entire jungle that filled up a warehouse. He even had an elephant. Big name entertainers, like Ben Vereen and The Commodores, sang the night away.

Ed picked me up in his customized Mercedes that night,

★

spending a lot of time answering his car phone as we drove. This was ten years ago, before every delivery boy in America owned one. And he was suave, he had all the lines.

We went to the Riviera, a little French place, and before we even got inside he spent a hundred dollars tipping the parking attendant to watch his Mercedes and the maitre d' to get us the choice table. Then he dropped three hundred more on wine. Oh he was pouring it on, chatting me up for all he was worth—he was worth several hundred million—and marching double time to get me. But I knew it wasn't me. It was the testosterone charge of scoring a Cheerleader. Like most Texas tycoons, he probably had a beach house, a private jet, and a yacht. He probably wanted to own a Cheerleader too. Who could blame him? We were "The 36 Most Beautiful Girls in Texas" and Texas had all the beautiful women. He was figuring I'd look awful good hanging on his arm at his next party.

And I probably would have, too, except "Fast Eddie" never stood a chance with me. I'd just met a guy named Hunt who kissed me and my heart short-circuited.

★

uzette and I joined the team just at the time when the Dallas Cowboys Cheerleaders were thrust into the world spotlight. In January 1976, at Super Bowl X in Miami, a Cheerleader named Gwenda Swearingen winked into a sidelines camera. That innocent little gesture started an explosion no one could have foreseen.

At that time, the world was ripe for All-American, girl next door, Texas-style sexiness. "The wink" became a part of the Cheerleader's folklore and sent a powerful message. One and a half billion people watching the telecast read that message loud and clear! Pittsburgh, the other team that went on to win Super Bowl X 21-17, didn't have cheerleaders, so the Cowboys Cheerleaders were highlighted throughout the game and broadcast throughout the world. *Dallas*, the TV show, would soon become an international smash and here came 36 dancing girls from Texas, American girls dressed up in showgirl Western outfits representing America's game and America's team. It was exactly what the world wanted to see.

In 1977, a poster of a group of Dallas Cowboys Cheerleaders in a sexy pose hit the market. It was snapped up almost before it could be put on the shelves and became one of the biggest selling posters of all time. It was everywhere that fall. It even outsold Farrah Fawcett. I remember going to a fraternity house at Texas Tech where I was a premed

★

student. The guys would all be watching the game and the poster would be plastered up behind the TV. They'd all be ooohing and aaahing over those Cheerleaders.

The whole world was mesmerized by the mystique of Texas. And with all of that sudden money Dallas was riding high in a state of euphoria. It was every legend, every tall tale of Texas come to life, and we represented that myth. We were the embodiment of the legendary Texas beauty; a team of Miss Americas.

The Cheerleaders were part of the glitzy glamour of Dallas. They represented the feeling of Texas at the time—that extravagance, that showy, look-at-me dazzle that is Dallas and Texas. We were the personification of the Texas Boom. But it felt more like a sonic boom.

During the years Suzette and I were Cheerleaders, a Fabergé shampoo commercial was made and the television special *The 36 Most Beautiful Girls in Texas* kicked off the Monday Night Football season. Mitsubishi took all the girls to Tokyo for two weeks to be a part of the Mirage Bowl. Another film, *Dallas Cowboys Cheerleaders, Part I*, was shot on location and became the second highest rated made-for-television movie in the history of the industry. It drew a 48 percent audience share. Suzette and I were chosen to represent the squad in an interview filmed with Sarah Purcell for *Real People,* and five of us were chosen to feud against five Dallas Cowboys on *Family Feud.* The Cheerleaders posed for a calendar, playing cards, frisbees, and a dozen other products. We performed at the 15th and 16th annual Academy of Country and Western Music Awards and at the Nashville Palace. We took part in another movie, *The Dallas Cowboys Cheerleaders, Part II*, and two episodes of *Love Boat.* We were featured in USO shows for troops all over the world, helped raise thousands of dollars for various char-

★

ities and telethons, and traveled from coast to coast performing at State Fairs and college half-time shows.

We were so hot we sizzled.

The Dallas Cowboys Cheerleaders were not just another cheerleading squad. No squad has ever had the exposure, the world-wide fame, the celebrity of the Dallas Cowboys Cheerleaders. We were a phenomenon; media darlings in every sense of the word.

After the game it was a high to come out of the tunnel into the parking lot and see thousands of fans waiting to get our autographs. They hung around for hours to see us. And they came from all over—busloads from every state in the union . . . Alaska, Connecticut, Wyoming, and even from Canada and Mexico. All to see a Cowboys game and, of course, to see those world-famous Cheerleaders. The Cowboys players and Cheerleaders dressed and exited on exact opposite sides of the stadium, so the people who lined up outside our tunnel were exclusively Dallas Cowboys Cheerleaders fans.

We performed at State Fairs where 300,000 people were spread out in an open field like at Woodstock or a Beach Boys concert. And we were the headliners, we were the show. We were all the way out in Spokane, Washington, at a shopping center and there were so many people we couldn't see the end of them. We could hardly breathe it was so crowded. And we signed autographs until our fingers were actually bleeding. At Westgate Mall in Spartanburg, South Carolina, 45,000 people clamored for autographs and a glimpse of a Cheerleader.

Wherever we went—Hawaii, Germany, Idaho, Japan—people flocked to see us. It amazed even us how big we were, especially outside of Texas. We were in Switzerland, for heaven's sake, and the president of the most powerful bank

★

in Switzerland, which of course, means one of the most important banks in the world, just melted at the sight of us. All he'd dreamed about for months was an autographed picture of the Dallas Cowboys Cheerleaders.

One man flew a group of Cheerleaders to Memphis to make an appearance at a huge indoor arena. The guy met the girls at the airport and took them all out to a fancy restaurant for lunch. Then he dropped them at their hotel. That night they got to the arena and there wasn't anyone there except eight or nine of his close buddies rolling around in this huge building that held about 10,000.

The guy hadn't advertised the Cheerleaders' appearance or let anyone know they were in town. He was loaded and just wanted to have his own little private personal appearance of the Dallas Cowboys Cheerleaders; just him and a few friends and the 12 most beautiful girls in Texas. Counting the cost of the appearance fee, the auditorium, airfares, hotel, and dinner, he probably dropped at least $50,000 for the privilege. . . . Never blinked an eye. But that's how it was. If you were a Dallas Cowboys Cheerleader you were a hot commodity in Dallas in those glory days. They'd do anything for you.

One Sunday morning *Louise Williams* couldn't find her uniform and realized in one horrifying moment that it was still at *Bob's Cleaning Emporium*. We were supposed to wash our uniform by hand but Louise broke the rule and took it to a professional dry cleaner. That put her in a full panic because if anything ever happened to a girl's uniform she was bounced off the team. No questions asked. She was just gone. We were never to let one of them out of our sight. And believe me, people would kill for one of the uniforms of the most famous group of girls in the world. In a survey conducted in Japan, the Dallas Cowboys Cheerleaders in uniform were recognized by more people than any other

★

females. Princess Di came in a distant second! And in those days Nancy Reagan was in another galaxy.

One girl left her uniform in her car and the car window was smashed and the uniform taken. She was immediately dismissed from the squad. The funny thing is, she had a new tape recorder sitting on the seat next to the uniform and the thief never even bothered about it. He wanted that uniform—with or without the girl in it. Of course, if he'd gotten a hold of it *with* the girl in it. . . . But that's another story.

So there was Louise down at Bob's Cleaning Emporium banging on the window like a complete mental case when a cop rolled by and did a U-turn and pulled right up next to her. "I left my uniform in there!" she screamed.

"Hold on there, young lady. What uniform?"

"My Cheerleader uniform. I've gotta get to the game!"

"The Cowboys game?"

"Yeah. I'm a Cowboys Cheerleader!"

"Well, we'll just have to break on in there then, won't we?"

Louise couldn't believe it. The cop went around back, took his night stick out and knocked a little hole in the back window. Then he reached in, opened it, and lifted this little bitty girl up and put her down inside the place. Louise ran over to where all the cleaned clothes were hanging on a revolving rack in alphabetical order. When she found the "W's" she started sorting through the hangers. Sure enough, there it was—the white hot pants, the royal blue top, and the white belt hanging down. So she grabbed her stuff, the cop lifted her back out the window, and she jumped in the car.

"Hurry on up now, ya hear," the cop said. "I know the boy who owns this place. I'll tell him what happened. He'll be braggin' on how one of you girls burgled his place."

A funny thing also happened to Suzette. She was a nursing student working at Baylor Hospital so, of course, she had

★

all the worst duties. She had to give enemas and empty bedpans and other things like that. And naturally it didn't take long before everybody on the ward knew she was a Dallas Cowboys Cheerleader.

One day, these two nice old ladies who'd been patients at Baylor spotted her at a shopping mall. She was walking on the ground level and the ladies were hanging over the rail of the level above.

"Suzette! Suzette!" They were yelling because they were a little deaf.

She stopped and looked up.

"You remember me, don't you," one of them yelled, at about a hundred decibels. "You're that nice Cowboys Cheerleader who gave me the enema last week."

It was a big deal even to get an enema from a Dallas Cowboys Cheerleader.

Whenever we made appearances in those days it almost always caused a near riot. The crowds went out of control. As soon as we stepped on stage screaming would erupt that wouldn't end until we were finished. This was the same kind of hysterical screaming and frenzy that had accompanied the Beatles or Elvis in their heyday. It was thrilling and downright scary at the same time.

On personal appearances Suzanne demanded that we be treated first class. And we loved it! Usually we were picked up in limos at the airport and whisked to the best hotel in town. Also, Suzanne charged a hefty fee of $500 a girl. The Cowboys organization gave us almost nothing, but as soon as someone else was paying for it, we got the best. It was part of our image. We were the best of the best. And Suzanne made them pay for the privilege of getting us.

Those personal appearances were our fun and our prize. And it was Suzanne who handed them out to reward us for

★

a job well done. Anyone who was on her bad list, which was long and complicated, stayed at home in Dallas. They ended up doing more free gigs than paid personal appearances.

Suzanne had a very tough set of criteria for promoters who wanted to hire us for a personal appearance. They had to furnish the license plate, make, and model of the car or limo that was supposed to pick us up. There had to be a minimum of two private security guards for the whole group and they had to furnish us with their names and badge numbers in advance. They had to furnish a typed, minute-by-minute itinerary of exactly where we were supposed to be. And the stage had to be a certain height, the hotel and airfare first class. By the time we arrived, our hosts had been made to feel as though they were receiving royalty.

Suzanne always gave the impression that everything was taken care of—that everything was under control and we were protected and always safe. But the fact is, we often found ourselves in extremely dangerous, out-of-control situations.

Once, in Waco, Texas, six of us went to a big VA hospital where there were lots of patients. The idea was to go in there, leave a poster and some autographed pictures, say hi, and leave. Just give them a little human contact.

When we got there, *Ginger Herrington* went up to a patient who was sitting off by himself.

"Hi! I'm Ginger. How are you?"

He didn't acknowledge her, instead just picked up a styrofoam cup and started shredding it.

Careene came over then so Ginger tried again.

"This is my friend Careene."

All of a sudden a nurse came running over and grabbed them both, pushed them away and screamed, "He's getting ready to attack. Move it!"

In another ward I went up to a patient lying in bed. He

★

was paralyzed from the waist down, was severely retarded, but was very big and had the upper body strength of a mature man. I leaned over him and said, "Hi, I'm Stephanie. I'm a Dallas Cowboys Cheerleader. What's your name?"

Suddenly he reached up, put his arms behind my neck, and pulled me down into his pillow. I instantly found myself in a jackknife position, my stomach crushed by the restraining bar of the bed. Both my legs were dangling in mid-air and there I was kicking and struggling to get free.

My whole face was buried in his pillow. I was being suffocated and I couldn't even scream for help. There was no one around; I really thought I was dead. Thank God Careene just happened to walk in the room. When she saw my legs kicking around in the air, she ran over and unlocked the guy's arms and I fell to the floor like a rag. I trembled for hours after the incident but never said a word to Suzanne. I knew it was part of my job. Frightening incidents like this came with the territory.

Crazy things happened constantly. Another time we appeared at the opening of a Southmark Mall in Omaha, Nebraska. People were crowded into every available space, even overflowing out the doors into the parking lot.

We were on the stage on the bottom floor of the mall and people were hanging over the second floor. They were supposed to line up for an autograph but instead the place turned into a riot. People were pushing from behind to try to get one of the pictures. Small children were being crushed against the stage and we had to grab them by the arms and haul them up onto the stage with us.

Ginger's father was at the top of the escalator with his video camera filming this incredible scene. Camcorders were rare back then. When he lifted the camera up to take a shot, a security guard mistook it for a weapon.

★

"Watch out!" the guard screamed. "He's got a gun!" And he pointed at Ginger's father.

A half-dozen policemen jumped on him and pushed him to the ground while Ginger watched in horror. She jumped out into the crowd and the mob just swallowed her up. Just like that, she was gone. Then suddenly she emerged, running up the escalator to get to her father.

"That's my father! That's my father!" she screamed. "Don't hurt him!"

That's the kind of crazy atmosphere that accompanied us everywhere. We never knew what was going to happen next.

The riot at the Tangerine Bowl was the scariest of all. The police came into our locker room after we had returned there following our half-time performance. "Folks, we've got a little problem here," they explained. "There's a mob of people out there and the only way we can get you to your bus is to hold hands, duck low, and we'll run with you."

We made our break while the majority of the fans were watching the second half of the game. The security guards locked arms with us so we could make a dash through the crowd that surrounded our bus.

The mob started tearing at us, trying to get at anything we were wearing. The worst problem though, was our hair. That's when it really got dangerous. When they pulled our hair, we couldn't move. Poor *Brandi Hardesty* had the most beautiful, long, blonde hair down past her waist, and a man got a hold of it as she tried to get by. She was stopped dead in her tracks, screaming for help. He had a pair of scissors and started cutting big chunks of it off. Finally, a policeman punched the guy and grabbed the scissors. Brandi got free but started crying, saying that her hair was her crowning glory.

The crowd of people just kept closing in, crushing us. The

★

security guards had to battle to get us out of there, beating back the crowd and pulling us by whatever they could get a hold of. When we were all finally on the bus, the driver slammed the door shut and took off. We all just looked around at each other in total shock.

We were just cheerleaders.

★

10

A Dallas Cowboys Cheerleader had to have her head screwed on awfully straight not to have it turned about by all the attention heaped upon her.

A girl auditioned for three weekends and if she made the team, the next day she was a celebrity. From a small town girl from Plano, Big Sandy, or Denison, to an international star put under a white-hot spotlight overnight.

Each girl handled her fame in her own way. A few of the girls tried never to let anyone know they were Cheerleaders. But many others used their fame like a passkey. They could get in any door in Texas with those three magic words—Dallas Cowboys Cheerleader.

"Oh, you're a Cheerleader. Come right in, little lady!"

There were rich men, fabulously rich men, all over Dallas and the Southwest who wanted to meet us, take us out, lavish us with anything our little hearts desired. Having a Dallas Cowboys Cheerleader on your arm was a coup, a male fantasy come to life.

Kim, Ginger, and Lisa were a few of the Cheerleaders who got swept up in the excitement and glamour of the experience. They were three beautiful girls all hyper and alive. No one could miss them.

Ginger was the ringleader. Ginger-a-go-go they called her. Everybody knew Ginger Herrington. There wasn't a single place, from the grocery store to the carwash, where some-

★

body didn't recognize Ginger. She had a very distinctive hairstyle, waist-length brown hair with a reddish tint that caught the sunlight, and squared-off bangs low to her eyebrows. Her hair sort of swished back and forth as she walked—because that's the way she walked; a lot of motion, shoulders back and a "watch out world" look on her face.

Ginger was the epitome of the little girl in a woman's body. And oh, my lord, could she dance. When she did it was like pure sex. She would put her whole body into everything she did. When she talked, her whole body was moving. When she laughed, the laughter would boom out of her and her hair would fly back, and she'd lean against you and laugh. Ginger never stopped. She danced like a demon at practice and games, then she'd dance all night at the clubs. She liked to get two or three of us out on the floor with her so we could draw a crowd. Then she'd put on a show. She had that distinctive hair and a devilish smile and the tightest little buns in the world. Everybody wanted to watch her and she wanted everybody to watch.

The three of them together were like nitro. There was nothing they couldn't do or get away with. If they wanted to dance on the tables, somebody would set them up for them. And dancing on tables was one of their specialties!

When they went into a disco or restaurant it was almost as if they owned the place. As soon as they walked in everybody knew who they were. They could never spend a cent, even if they tried. There was no way for them to keep up with all the drinks people were buying them. They'd all be drunk in an hour, and when they'd leave the place, a half dozen full drinks were left untouched. For them to go out and drink three bottles of champagne that cost $200 apiece was nothing. It happened two or three times a week. Every night if they wanted.

They'd go to the most expensive restaurant in town with

★

pennies in their purses and never worry about the check. They knew they'd never see a check. Men would fight over it.

"No, this is my check, buddy!"

"Forget it! I've been waiting for years to buy dinner for a Cheerleader and I'm doing it, damn it!"

That's the way it went every night.

Just four years before, Kim was a little girl from Taiwan who couldn't speak the language, and now the whole world was laid at her feet—what power! The minute a guy found out she was a Cheerleader, it was like an aphrodisiac to him. She could be standing next to a dead ringer for Christie Brinkley, but all he'd see would be Kim.

Kim quickly realized how valuable her beauty and her celebrity were and what amazing things it could do. There was big money everywhere in Dallas and as she strolled through town men literally showered her with it.

Before, she would see a cute guy and go moony-eyed, and he'd pick her up for a date in a baseball cap and a T-shirt and they'd grab a burger. But overnight, she realized there were other men; wealthy older men who wanted to give her things and take her to exciting places. When one of these men asked Kim out to dinner, he was likely to pick her up in his Lear jet and take her to New Orleans just because one time she'd said she liked Cajun food.

Kim could see that if she wanted to receive nice things, the world was at her fingertips. She'd go by limo to the fanciest restaurants in town and the guy would order enough food to feed ten people.

"Have you ever tried truffles?"

"No. What's it like?"

"Well, let's find out. Waiter! Bring this beautiful lady an order of truffles."

This was the first time Kim had ever been out of the house

★

living by herself and she'd gone wild. She went out with Ginger and Lisa one night and drank more tequila than she'd bargained for. . . . A lot more. In no time, Kim's brains were whirling. She felt like she had a fish bowl on her head and the fish were still in it swimming around. Cafe Dallas had this deal going. If you drank twelve shots, you got to keep the shot glass. And Kim wanted that glass. So everybody kept feeding her those tequila shots and she was sinking fast. There were twenty guys there that would have bought every glass in the place for her, if she'd given the word. But that was no fun.

Kim didn't remember getting home that night from Cafe Dallas, but around eleven in the morning the phone rang.

"I think you have my shoes," Lisa said.

Kim looked down. She was still fully dressed with her purse still slung over her shoulder and sure enough, there were Lisa's shoes on her feet.

"I got a question," Kim said. "I wear a size five. What size are these shoes?"

"Eight."

"How in the hell did I get up the two flights of stairs to my apartment dead drunk in size eight shoes without breaking my neck?"

"Miracles happen. What time do I pick you up?"

"Huh?"

"There's a great new Chinese joint out by my place. I'll pick you up for lunch. Half hour, okay."

"Okay."

After they ate, they went to Happy Hour at Friday's and started all over again.

Bobby Sue couldn't understand how the girls like Kim and Lisa and Ginger—and Inger and Zee and several others—went out every night like that. Bobby Sue would go to work

★

all day and rush home, throw on her only dance outfit and rush to practice. She'd get home at midnight or one or two and fall into her bed just to get up at 6:30 the next morning and start all over. After she paid for the rent, utilities, gasoline, makeup, and pantyhose, none of which was reimbursed by the Cowboys, she had 85 cents a day to live on. So the staples of her diet were Diet Cokes and peanut butter.

But Lisa, Kim, Ginger, Inger, and several others would go out every night after practice and come home at five or six in the morning, if they made it home at all. They seemed to have boundless energy. They'd come home from practice at midnight and get dressed and go out dancing—*every night*. On top of that, they always had great clothes, a nice place to live and they seemed to have a new car about every six months. None of the girls except the Scholz sisters and one or two of the other girls came from wealthy families. Most of them were dirt poor just like Bobby Sue and came from paycheck-to-paycheck families. So how did they do it?

One night, Bobby Sue was sitting on the floor of the apartment that she shared with three other girls, counting her money: "86, 87, 88 . . ." It was Tuesday. She got paid on Friday and she had 88 cents to live on until then.

Suzanne Mitchell worked us so hard that practically all our energy went into being Cheerleaders. We were paid fifteen dollars a game. And we had to look like ramp models when we went to the 7-11 for a loaf of bread. The amount of makeup and clothes needed to keep up that image were astronomical. But we had to look great or we were off the team. The only problem was that there never seemed to be enough time or means or energy to do it all. Where they thought a full-time job was going to fit into all of this, Bobby Sue could never figure out.

She was completely exhausted from the schedule. She

★

wasn't sleeping and she didn't have any gas for her car. Bobby Sue sat there counting her money that evening and then she started crying.

Matters were only going to get worse financially for Bobby Sue. After her appearance as a primary character on an episode of "Love Boat," she was kicked out of the apartment by an envious roommate. Bobby Sue had spent three nights in her car when the man for whom she worked expressed concern about how tired she looked. When he heard where she'd been sleeping he gave her a key to his home. Upon arriving that night she found a room of her own prepared by his wife. The family bought Bobby Sue new clothes and accepted her as their own. She felt grateful, particularly since she couldn't ask for help from her own family. She knew they had no money to spare and she didn't want them to worry about her.

Bobby Sue, like most of the girls, knew a way to solve the money problem. His name was *Greg*. He was a guardian angel to many of the girls, generously helping them out in their time of need. Zee, for example, had nothing more than a bed in the apartment she rented. One day, when she came home from work, she found it filled with about $600 worth of rental furniture supplied by Greg. But Bobby Sue just couldn't call Greg. She didn't operate that way.

Greg loved being surrounded by Cheerleaders. Many of the girls, like Ginger, Inger, *Trudi*, Zee, and Lisa and Kim accepted his gifts and his help. Greg was very generous. He loved to see the girls have fun. And he was nice. He never asked for anything. He just loved being around the girls. Bobby Sue was always non-judgmental about Greg and the other girls, but when one of them drove up to practice in a brand new car, she knew where it had come from.

"You know I'm not from a rich family like yours," Bobby Sue once told me. "These girls have fur coats and jewelry.

★

They have all these things to make them gorgeous. Things! I'm not used to things. When I grew up I got things like thongs. Every summer I got a new pair of thongs. Suzanne told me to get my roots dyed the other day. That's sixty dollars. Where am I going to get that money? I can't compete."

Bobby Sue's best friend on the squad was Zee. And they were a very odd couple. Zee was wild and gutsy. . . . She'd try anything. Nobody could keep up with Zee. She was so much more experienced than the rest of us that we found her shocking. But Bobby Sue just loved her because she *was* so outrageous, so completely different from her.

Zee was married and was having an affair with a neighbor. Then she had another boyfriend in Dallas. Most of us had been brought up in Baptist homes where it was a sin to dance with a boy. Zee was older, had been married, had had two or three affairs, and had slept with a man strictly for sex. (Most of us had still not even seen a man naked before, much less had a hot, sexual affair with one.)

Zee, along with Starr, became our sexual advisors and before Starr was cut from the squad we had all learned a lot. They drew diagrams and everything.

One day at practice, we were lined up in the tunnel waiting for Suzanne to put the music on so we could go through our routine again for about the twentieth time. It seems there were always "Masters and Johnson" debates going on during those times in the tunnel. On this particular day someone brought up the question of oral sex.

"What's oral sex?" Zee chimed in. "Well, I'll tell you."

Every girl within earshot tuned in.

"Are you holding onto something?" asked Zee. And she proceeded to give us her explanation in explicit detail.

Bobby Sue couldn't believe what she was hearing. "But don't they go to the bathroom with it?"

★

DEEP IN THE HEART OF TEXAS

"Among other things," Zee laughed.

Zee and Starr would regale us with their sexual escapades by the hour. Zee knew she had our undivided attention that day in the tunnel, so she continued.

"The closest thing to an orgasm is a max takeoff in a Gulfstream G-2 aircraft. A max takeoff is when you taxi onto the runway, apply full brakes, and run the engines all the way up. Those planes've got Rolls Royce engines so they scream like a banshee as they accelerate. They start off with a slow roar, increase slowly, and finish with a high-pitched scream. It's scary. Oh baby! The whole plane shudders with excitement, then the pilot lets go of the brakes, and whoosh, you rocket right out of there!

"*Jeff* said the ultimate would be if we had sex during a max takeoff. So that's what we did."

"You did?"

"Yep. Jeff got his co-pilot to pilot the plane and we started playing around in the back as he taxied out. We were really getting hot and as we shot down the runway, Jeff screamed, 'Take off!' "

"Reeeallly!"

"I nearly passed out."

Zee was the kind of girl who would try anything. She had the nerve of a fighter pilot.

One Tuesday night Suzanne told Zee that she was going to be featured on the next "Cowboys Weekly" TV show because she was a pilot. Suzanne wanted her to take the airplane up and buzz it around and maybe throw in a few little tricks to add some excitement. That was Tuesday and they were going to film on Saturday.

Well, Zee had lied just a little bit on her Cheerleader resumé. She had stood up at the tryouts and told the judges she had a pilot's license and was studying to be a commercial pilot. And she meant every word of it. Actually, she didn't

★

Suzette, Sheri, and Stephanie (clockwise from left) in cheerleading costumes of their own design, 1990.

Mother, always the perfect model. December 1962.

Daddy got a football scholarship to Baylor. When he transferred to Texas A & I in Kingsville, he was nominated for Little All American halfback.

Suzette's first dance recital in Dallas when she was four years old.

Stephanie, eleven years old, with her winning trophies at the Texas State Championship Twirling contest held in Dallas in 1971.

Sheri as a contestant in a beauty pageant at six years of age in 1972.

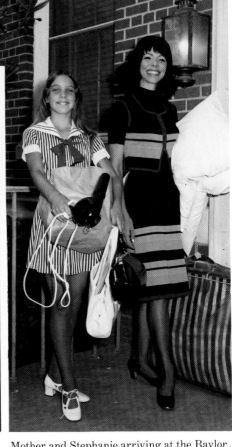

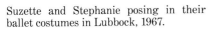
Suzette and Stephanie posing in their ballet costumes in Lubbock, 1967.

Mother and Stephanie arriving at the Baylor University dormitory for the "Our Little Miss Texas" pageant in 1972. *(Photo by Richard Jackson)*

Sheri Scholz, Miss Texas Teen U.S.A. in 1984. *(Photo by Suddarth)*

We were all members of the Coronado High School Varsity Cheerleading Squad in Lubbock. Sheri (above) in 1984; Suzette (left) in a nostalgic 1950s pep rally outfit in 1976; Stephanie (right) in 1977.

Suzette in her famous canary yellow outfit at the Dallas Cowboys Cheerleaders tryouts in 1978. *(Photograph by David Woo/Dallas Morning News)*

Suzette posing
with Spiderman.

Stephanie in action one blistering hot afternoon in Texas Stadium.

Suzette signing her much sought-after autograph for an adoring fan, with an ever-present security guard.

Sheri singing the national anthem before a game in 1985.

Dallas Cowboys Cheerleaders appeared in a variety of benefit shows both live and on national television. With the Oak Ridge Boys at Stars for Children benefit 1979 (top); with Dallas Cowboys players on "Family Feud" for the Boys and Girls Clubs of America (middle); and, on the Variety Club Telethon with coach Tom Landry in 1979 (bottom).

Suzette (at right) along with other cheerleaders executing one of their typical sideline routines.

Suzanne Mitchell, former Dallas Cowboys Cheerleaders Director dressed up for one of the Show Group's personal appearances.

Texie Waterman, our top-rated choreographer, alerting us that it's "showtime!" at a State Fair performance in the early 1980s.

Stephanie in action on the field. *(Photo by David Woo*/Dallas Morning News*)*

We made a lot of personal appearances such as visits to St. Jude's Children Research Hospital in Memphis, Tennessee in 1980 (top) and the Korea U.S.O. Christmas tour in 1980 (right).

The very first Dallas Cowboys Cheerleaders reunion held December 2, 1989.

It seems there were a lot of celebrities around and here Bob Hope finds himself in the midst of all of us, 1981.

Suzette and Barbara Mandrell, 1981.

Three generations of Texas women: Suzette, Mamie, Sheri, Stephanie, and Mother, 1981. *(Photo by Michael Connors)*

Bill, Catherine, and Sheri. *(Photo by Jim Allen)*

Capri, Stephanie, Noelle, Hunt, and Tiffany *(Photo by Bob Mader)*

Butch, Dustin, Chase, and Suzette *(Photo by Jim Allen)*

have the license in her hand, but she'd passed all the written tests and all the other red tape. All she needed to do was take her final test flight. But that took money and right at the moment, she didn't have it.

So, Zee could go up and do her solo flying but she couldn't actually take any passengers, and there was supposed to be a cameraman and a program emcee in the plane with her as they shot footage for the show. Zee had lied herself into a pretty big corner and if Suzanne found out, she'd kill her.

Wednesday morning Zee got on the phone to the Arlington Airport and said, "I've got to get my license. The problem is I haven't flown in six months. I'm a good pilot but haven't flown recently. And I've got to have my license by Saturday morning because I'm going to be flying on a TV show on Saturday afternoon."

"Well, that's a pretty tight schedule there lady. You can't just—"

"You don't understand. I'm a Dallas Cowboys Cheerleader and—"

"You're a Cheerleader? Oh, why didn't you say so. Hell, yes, we can open up our schedule and help you make your deadline. Tell you what, since you're an accomplished flyer, you bring an autographed picture and I'll make sure of a smooth ride. That a deal?"

"Oh, that's great!"

"Just ask for *George*."

"Thank you, George."

"You bet."

Zee had to borrow the three hundred from Greg for the testing and licensing. After a good laugh, he lent her the money. She raced down to the airport and George took her right up.

The weather had been lousy all week. Zee had to do all the routine stuff, which was easy enough in good weather

★

but difficult in turbulent conditions. But in that weather she couldn't control a thing. She was all over the damn sky, bouncing around, with thunderheads going off in the distance. On top of that, she'd done all her previous flying in a Cessna 150 but all they had available in Arlington was a Cessna 172. There's a big difference in the two planes, so when Zee tried to fly she was lost. She ended up having to stay in Arlington all day Wednesday, Thursday, and Friday fighting that plane.

Saturday, at dawn, it was clear as a bell. Zee went up with the FAA examiner and she did everything perfectly. A guardian angel was smiling down on her. She landed and George said, "Well Sandy, you could use some polish in a couple of areas. But I'm gonna pass you. Congratulations."

He signed her off and she was an official pilot. She hugged George and gave him a big kiss. Fantastic!

It was twelve o'clock. The film crew from the Cowboys Weekly showed up at one. And off they went into the very wild blue yonder. Only they didn't know just how wild.

Oh, but Zee did put on a show for them. They were in the back all smiling away, confident they were in the hands of an old pro. The way Suzanne had been P.R.ing Zee, they thought they were flying with Amelia Earhart. She was leaning back, smiling into the camera, flying one-handed while they interviewed her, reminiscing about all the adventures she'd had flying. By the time she was through, they thought Zee was a WWII flying ace and a 747 pilot all rolled into one.

After the flight she brought the plane back around and kissed that baby down right on the runway, the cameras rolling the whole way. It was all perfect.

Only Zee could have pulled it off.

One morning Greg called Zee. "I'll pick you up in ten minutes. Meet me out in front of your apartment."

★

"Where're we going?"

"Shopping."

Zee threw on something and went outside. As she was looking up and down the street for Greg's car, a black Lincoln pulled up to the curb next to her.

The window rolled down and Greg stuck his head out.

"Get in."

"What's all this?"

"Our magic carpet for the day. We're going to Neiman Marcus so I can buy you something to wear to the party tonight."

That day they drove all over Dallas—to downtown Neiman's, to Lou Lattimore's, to the Highland Park boutiques—drinking margaritas and eating caviar. Before it was over, Greg had spent several thousand dollars on Zee. It was a fantasy and she never wanted to wake up.

Later, Greg dropped Zee off at her apartment and yelled out the car window, "I'll pick you up at 7:30. I know you'll look fabulous." How could she look anything but fabulous with all those beautiful clothes.

When Greg picked Zee up that night, everybody was already in the limo. Kim and Lisa and Inger and Trudi and *Debi* and Ginger. All of them drinking and looking fabulous. All of them dressed up in expensive clothes with jewelry sparkling everywhere.

Greg loved to have a beautiful woman on his arm. He loved the fantasy of people thinking he was going home with these girls. He'd walk into a party with five or six of the Cheerleaders and everyone wanted to know who he was.

"Greg was always luring the girls to parties," Bobby Sue told me. "He piled gifts on everyone but never really asked for anything in return."

When Greg was going to a party, whoever got the call would go with him, along with three or four other Cheer-

★

leaders, and he'd be happy. And the girls would be happy too, because the parties were the best in Dallas—catered with caviar and giant shrimp and Russian Vodka. It was like being on *Dynasty*. Rich and handsome men were everywhere. Just the kind their mothers said to bring home.

Greg had a lot of rich and influential friends. He'd set one of the girls up on a blind date and the guy would own half of Ohio.

A lot of the girls ended up being supported by rich men. Most of them had been given "jobs" in which they didn't do anything. One man was in the clothing business and he hired several of the girls to model for him at four times the going rate. They'd make a thousand or two a day! The modeling agencies would send them to a convention where the men thought they were geishas and they'd get eighty dollars and a hundred pawings. But this man took the girls to New York and rented apartments for them and they flew in and out whenever they wanted. They would have been crazy not to accept.

The owner of one of the Dallas radio stations liked taking care of the girls. He was very wealthy and very handsome. He had lunch everyday at Fridays and there were always Cheerleaders at the table with him. He'd pay them just to be there. Four, five hundred here and there, just to be seen with him. And, of course, to come by his house.

Another man hired Joy to work for him for $3,500 a month. She'd been working at *Ribbons and Lace*, a dress shop, for minimum wage. But thanks to being a Cheerleader, Joy went from a $6,000 a year job to a $40,000 a year job. That's all it took. She worked for him for three years and she never knew what her job was. He'd get her to get autographed pictures of the squad. But not much else. She didn't have regular hours and she never did much. But every month she'd pick up her $3,500.

★

He also bought her clothes, diamond earrings, and lots of other things. If there was a party coming up, he'd say, "Here's $500, go get a dress."

How could she say no? She was like a Barbie doll. She liked the attention and the feeling of being taken care of.

Chantelle had seen more of life than the rest of us. She wasn't all wrapped up in the same illusions that we were. She loved the Cheerleaders but she saw it more as a great opportunity for fun and fortune. She knew how to handle Suzanne and she knew how to handle men. Boy, did she know how to handle men!

Chantelle wouldn't let herself fall in love. The first time she had, she married the guy. He turned out to be a real loser. When she got out of that relationship, look out! Men were not going to get close to her.

After her marriage she dated only wealthy men—wealthy, generous men. Chantelle's number in our USO Shows was "Hey Big Spender" and it was strictly type casting. "If you don't have the money, honey, I haven't got the time."

She had a list of men she called her "Ten Most Wanted List." If a man didn't have lots of money and shower her with gifts—diamonds, jewelry, and cars—he was not considered in her "Top Three." There was never a "Top One." It was always a one, two, and three. And they shuffled around and dropped out of those exalted spots at her whim. Of course, a Mercedes on her birthday might catapult some lowly sucker right back on top in a hurry, but not necessarily.

"Honey, he's number one now. But he better keep working hard or he'll be number three in a flash!"

When Greg and his limo filled with Cheerleaders pulled up to the party that night, Chantelle was already there.

"Chantellllllle!" Lisa squealed, as she ran over and hugged her.

"How do you find these parties?" Lisa asked. But she knew

★

the answer already. Chantelle claimed she had a built-in early warning device for rich men.

"If they're out there, I'll find them," she laughed.

Then Chantelle spotted Cooki Simms. She grabbed Cooki's arm and off they went. Before the night was through, Cooki was offered two new cars, a trip to Jamaica, and a new apartment. But not one indecent proposal. They were going to just give it to her.

"I don't understand it Chantelle. They don't ask for anything."

"Girl, you're not dealing with cab drivers here. They don't just drive right up and expect a tip. These men are developers."

"Developers?"

"Yes, maam! You're dealing with class. Before these guys build a home, they put in the pavement. That trip to the Caribbean? That's the ground-breaking ceremony. And that new BMW? That's the driveway to your heart."

Cooki laughed.

"But, honey, tell 'em to forget about the apartment."

"Oh?"

"Yes, maam. He can have the key to your heart. But don't ever let him have the key to your place."

★

t our very first Cheerleaders meeting, Suzanne came into the room and flipped on a movie projector. For about ten minutes she played clips of a game from the year before. When the film was finished she turned the camera off and flipped on the lights.

"Now who knows why I showed you this film?" she asked.

"To show us the excitement of Dallas Cowboys football?"

"No. Anyone else?"

"To show us what it's like to be at a game."

"No. This film is to show you what's off limits. This is the closest you'll ever get to the players."

That's when we learned it was strictly against team rules to date a player. If a Cheerleader was caught "fraternizing" with a Cowboy, no matter how innocently, she was immediately cut from the squad. The truth is, there wasn't that much fraternizing between players and Cheerleaders. Frankly, most of the girls weren't attracted to any of them. There were too many wealthy, attractive, and intelligent men hovering around us. There were some girls who broke the rules, however. A few of the Cheerleaders *were* sleeping with Cowboys—but only a few. One of the players and a Cheerleader who were dating for a while actually had signals worked out so they could communicate during the games. He'd kneel and hold his helmet a certain way if they were going to meet after the game, and she would wig-wag back an answer with her pom-poms in their own secret semaphore.

★

DEEP IN THE HEART OF TEXAS

Most of the girls were privy to the code, and sometimes her whole group would answer him. Nothing like teamwork.

At one particular game, a cameraman unknowingly caught the player in the act. The photo appeared that week with a caption attributing the player's smile to one of his outstanding plays. There he was, with that special hold on his helmet, grinning away as he was taking in his honey's message. We laughed about that one for weeks.

Over the years there were quite a few "bad boys" on the Cowboys—boys who had developed their own special reputation among the Cheerleaders. We stayed informed of those players and tried to avoid them. Remember, we had all been specifically told that if we were ever caught in what even appeared to be a compromising position with a player, it was the Cheerleader who would lose the most by being immediately dismissed.

The only one of the Dallas Cowboys who ever put me in an uncomfortable position was Danny White. It happened when I appeared on *The Family Feud* with five Cowboys—Danny, Tony Dorsett, Larry Cole, Harvey Martin, and Charlie Waters—and four other Cheerleaders.

We feuded against the players for the Boys and Girls Clubs of America and we filmed all five shows in one day. That's a lot of "Good answer! Good answer!" for one day, but it was great fun. And very exciting, too, because there was plenty of obvious electricity between us.

Between shows, all ten of us were in one dressing room relaxing, recurling our hair, and reapplying makeup for the tenth time. The players, of course, were trying to make us laugh, flirting like mad, the conversation always dancing on the outskirts of sex.

By the end of the day we were all very comfortable with one another and the guys had become more familiar with

★

us—all in a friendly way . . . you know, a little pat after a joke, or a hand on a shoulder when they handed us a soft drink. It's all part of the standard ritual between boys and girls.

Well, Danny went beyond the standard ritual. I was in the hallway. He came up from behind me, put his arms around me, and squeezed tightly, as only a football player can.

"Don't you know that dynamite comes in small packages," he whispered.

I didn't really know how to handle the situation. I couldn't tell whether Danny was serious or just flirting, but it made me uncomfortable. I was petrified Suzanne might have seen it happen and think I had condoned it. I broke out of his arms, turned around, gave him the dirtiest look I could muster, and hissed, "Hands off, buddy!"

Danny was very good looking and self assured. On top of that he had a good sense of humor. I like a man who can make me laugh. But my number one taboo was that I didn't date married men.

The most infamous story that passed through our ranks about a member of the football team had to do with a particular Cowboy who was late for the team plane leaving for an important game one year. Word was that he had been ensconced with a Cheerleader. Some reports even alluded to his being fined a hefty sum for his tardiness.

Afterwards, one of our squad members joked, "Heck, I would have fulfilled his fantasy but gotten him to the airport before the plane was scheduled to leave, and charged him a good deal less than he was fined. He could have saved money and probably had a better time."

"Oh, I can beat that," another girl jumped in. "For an even bigger discount, I would have let you take care of him but I would have monitored the clock for you both so I could

★

pick him up and deliver him to the airport in plenty of time. That way he gets everything he wants and saves a lot more money and I wouldn't have to do anything but be a chauffeur."

The Dallas Cowboys and their Cheerleaders—the essence of machismo and glamour to sports fans—were not only America's favorites, but epitomized teamwork to the hilt.

★

12

The only thing that saved Suzette and me, and later Sheri, from the temptation that many of the other girls fell prey to, was that we were chaperoned through life. We were protected by my mother's vigilance and my father's money. Even after we'd left the house, Mother called every day and every night. They paid for everything—our food, our apartment, our clothes, gas, and car . . . everything. And they watched us like a couple of prairie hawks.

Our family was always our safety net. If we fell we knew we were going to get caught. We knew somebody would be there to help or listen, somebody to cry with when things were bad. So many of the other girls had families that didn't care. It's a miracle they didn't all get lost and fall prey to the organization and the many temptations all around them.

My mother and father were always dropping in unexpectedly to the apartment that Suzette and I shared in Dallas. So I wasn't completely surprised when they showed up unannounced one Saturday.

"Oh, hi Mother, hi Daddy."

"Hi, honey. Where's Suzette?"

"Oh, she's on a personal appearance."

Actually, she had driven to St. Louis with her boyfriend, Butch. Butch and Suzette would eventually get married the next year but at that time they weren't even engaged yet.

The whole goal of my mother's Master Plan was to get us

★

married to an ambitious man, somebody who would take good care of us and who could eventually provide us with a comfortable life. A major component of this strategy was to get us married early so no disaster would happen before we could make it to the altar and say, "I do."

Mother was certain that if one of her girls slept with a man, he would never marry her because she would no longer be a virgin. She wouldn't be "perfect." The longer a girl waited to get married, the greater the risk she ran of losing her virginity.

I remember my mother saying to Mamie at Suzette's wedding, "Well, that's one we don't have to worry about anymore. One down, two to go."

That morning when I told her Suzette was away on a personal appearance, my mother slipped into Suzette's bedroom and went through her closets. She discovered that her Cheerleader uniform was still hanging in there.

She came busting into the living room a second later.

"You're lying to me, Stephanie."

"What do you mean?"

"Her uniform's still in her closet. Where is she?"

Suzette and I had a solemn pact never to rat on each other and had covered for each other a thousand times. Mother kept grilling me but I played stupid. So they sat there and waited for Suzette to show up. Mother camped herself on the couch while Daddy wore out the carpet for twelve hours, from nine in the morning until nine that night, when Suzette and Butch finally strolled in the door.

It took our parents about a minute to find out where they'd been. My mother lit all over Suzette and my father went after Butch.

"What the hell do you think you're doing taking my daughter out of town like that?"

"I'm sorry Dr. Scholz."

★

"Don't tell me you're sorry. You stay away from my daughter."

It went on that way for a couple of hours before Suzette and Butch calmed them down. But it was only after Butch made known his intention to marry Suzette.

"Who says we want you to marry her?" Daddy asked.

But that was a bluff. When he'd found out Suzette was serious about Butch, he'd had detectives run a few checks on him—credit report, woman report, past marriages or kids he wasn't letting on to. Butch passed with flying colors. Plus, he was a surgeon over at Baylor.

Start printing the invitations!

When we were growing up, Suzette, Sheri, and I were probably best described as prudes. We were preached to over and over that the one golden rule of dating was to not let anyone take away our virginity unless we had a marriage license in hand and a ring on our finger.

Suzette and I had a pact. If one of us was out on a date with someone and he got out of hand, she could call the other sister to come pick her up.

When Suzette and I were roommates at Texas Tech, we went out with most of the guys on campus at least once. I can remember going on dates with a number of wolves and when they would get a little too frisky I'd say, "Excuse me, I need to go to the bathroom." I'd go to the nearest phone and call Suzette and she'd come and get me. The guy would never see me again.

When we began dating, Daddy had been like a grizzly bear when it came to our boyfriends. My parents' curfew was 11:00, but we had always pushed it. Even if we were sitting out front in the car they'd flip the porch light on and off which meant we'd better get our tail feathers in pretty fast.

One night Suzette was parked in front of our house with her high school sweetheart. It was late, about 1 A.M. Daddy

★

must have heard the car pull up and the engine go off. But because Suzette was supposed to have been in already he thought it was a burglar. So he got his big-time shotgun, loaded it, came outside in his underwear, and pointed the barrel of his bazooka at the car.

When he realized who was in the car, he started yelling at Suzette to get her little butt in the house. And he told the guy, "Don't ever come back to this house again, boy!" All the time pointing that shotgun at him.

Guys were terrified of my father. He had this way of intimidating boys when they came to the house. It made them think twice about trying anything with his girls.

My mother's way of keeping us pure was to set us up with nerds.

On Suzette's first date she was taken to the Stardust Ball. The boy that took her thought the music was too loud, which is something you'd expect to hear from a grandparent, not from a sixteen-year-old guy. To muffle the music he stuck cotton in his ears. When that didn't work, he stuffed more cotton in there. By the time they went out to dance he had these great muffs of cotton sticking out of his ears.

The worst, however, was yet to come. Suzette's date had stuffed the cotton so far into his ears that a lot of it got stuck. So my father had to drive down to the dance where the poor guy was reeling in agony on the back seat of his parents' borrowed car and remove the cotton from his ears.

Another one of my mother's strategies was to keep us so busy with dance lessons and extracurricular activities that we didn't have time to get into mischief. Plus, she always knew where we were and who we were with. All the kids would come to our house. It was the hangout for our gang. Mother would always have popcorn or sweets on hand and everyone was welcome, so they wanted to come back.

If she heard us whispering that we were going to toilet

★

paper a house, my mother would say, "Okay, I'll take you." And she would. We'd all drive to the store to buy the t.p. and then drive over to the victim's house, and my mother would wait in the car while we did our dirty work.

The way she protected us was very clever. It never really dawned on me until I had children of my own.

Of course the drawback to all this vigilance was that it could become counterproductive as we neared the altar with our intended.

After my husband, Hunt, asked me to marry him, he wanted to get my father's formal permission. It's the way men handle things in the South.

We were all staying in a cabin out in West Texas. Hunt and Daddy went on one of their bird hunting trips at this place near Lubbock called Duck Creek. There were lots of plump birds flying around slower than a dog with wings out there. And all morning Hunt and Daddy just shot the hell out of those birds.

About the time they were going to call it quits, Hunt shot a bird and the dog brought it over and put it at Hunt's feet. He picked it up and handed it to Daddy.

"Ken, I want to marry your daughter." He had his shotgun resting in the crook of his elbow. My father had his at his side.

"How're you figuring on taking care of her? She's expensive. How are you going to support her habit of matching shoes and bag? You need to get a residency when you finish school."

"I'll get a residency. I'll be a plastic surgeon and I'll be able to provide well for her."

Daddy kind of scratched his jaw a little and looked down at his gun. Then he picked it up and blew a bird out of the sky. He liked Hunt a lot.

"Okay. Let's go on up to the cabin and we'll talk about it."

★

DEEP IN THE HEART OF TEXAS

The next morning my mother came into the living room of the cabin we were staying in. She'd heard the good news and was planning a little celebration that night at the fanciest restaurant around. The problem was, Hunt was a med student, so he was poorer than a boondog.

"Hunt, honey," she said, "after we drive back to Lubbock today, I want to take you up to Latham's and buy you some clothes. We're taking you out tonight and I want you to have something special to wear."

Hunt had to sit down and almost put his head between his legs because of the way the blood seemed to rush out of his body. How in the world could a man keep his independence and freedom if his mother-in-law was going to spend thousands to outfit him?

After thinking it over, Hunt swallowed his pride and decided to go along with Mother for the ride. He had never in his life gone on a shopping spree like this one—new boots, new pants, new sports jackets and ties, and even a new suede vest and hat.

That night we celebrated at the Lubbock Club and Hunt looked like a million bucks. The clothes didn't really matter to either of us. He always looked so handsome to me. We were madly in love with one another, and just wanted to be in each other's arms and spend the rest of our lives together.

I knew my search was over. Hunt had found the key to my heart.

★

oni Wallace was one of the friendliest girls on our squad. If anybody needed anything she was there to help out. She worked at *Rodeo Roundup*, a Country and Western bar and restaurant. It was a real dive. A bunch of the Cheerleaders used to like to get decked out in suede and leather Western wear with our fanciest boots and hats on. Then we'd go to Rodeo Roundup dressed in our five-hundred-dollar outfits while everybody else was in jeans.

Loni worked as a hostess. When we arrived she'd give us the best table.

That's where she met *Johnny Robinson*, and that changed her life completely.

One day a good-looking man wearing shorts came to the door.

"You can't come in here with those shorts on."

"What?"

"No shorts allowed."

He laughed at her and kept walking through the door. So she grabbed his arm.

"I'm serious."

"Do you know who I am?"

"Sure, you're a guy wearing shorts and you can't come in."

"I'm one of the owners of this place."

★

"That's nice, but you're still not getting in with those shorts on."

"But I just got back from a fishing trip."

"That's nice. But no shorts."

One of the bartenders came out. "Any problem Loni? Oh, Mr. Robinson, I didn't recognize you sir. How was the fishing trip?"

"Just great. Thanks *Bert*."

"You really do own this place," Loni sighed.

"Yeah." And he offered his hand to shake. "My name's Johnny Robinson."

"Nice to meet you. But you still can't come in with those shorts on. It's bad for business."

"You know you're right. I've got a pair of pants in my office. Can I stay if I go in and put them on?"

"That's a deal," Loni said, and they both laughed.

Loni had a face like Ginger Rogers and a build like an Olympic swimmer complete with wide shoulders, pinched waist, and muscular thighs. She had natural white-blonde hair and aquamarine eyes and always had a deep tan. Loni looked like the kind of girl the Beach Boys sang about.

Johnny came back later in the evening.

"I want to take you out," he said.

"I don't date people I work with."

He grinned.

"But you don't work with me. You work for me."

"Doesn't make any difference."

Johnny tried a little more and they laughed a little more and, finally, he gave up.

Later that night Loni was talking with one of the other girls who worked at the restaurant.

"Don't you realize how much money that guy's got? He owns his own multimillion-dollar company. And a bunch of restaurants.

★

"Doesn't make any difference. I don't date people I work with."

A couple of weeks later, Loni got an offer to work at a restaurant that was more upscale. The day she quit her job at Rodeo Roundup, Johnny called her.

"I'm picking you up for dinner."

"What?"

"7:30 okay?"

"Who is this?"

"Johnny."

"Johnny Robinson? You sure don't waste any time."

"Life is short. 7:30?"

"Why not."

Johnny picked Loni up in a white stretch Cadillac wearing a coyote fur coat. He had on cream-colored, snakeskin boots and there were rings on all his fingers. Crowning him was a brown suede cowboy hat with a falcon feather in the band. When she opened the door, Loni went into shock. He looked like a pimp.

Back then the prestige spot in Dallas was the Reunion Tower. The whole place revolved, giving diners a 360 degree view of the city. That night, Johnny chauffeured Loni over to Reunion Tower and swept her in. He knew everybody. At the door, he slipped the maitre d' a fifty and he glided them over to a table in the quietest corner with the best view. From the minute they sat down they laughed. Johnny told stories about fishing trips in the Caribbean. No bragging or boasting; he wasn't that way, but he was flamboyant. Wherever he went people knew he was there but not because he'd spend all night talking about himself.

At the end of the evening Johnny took Loni home. Not even a kiss at the door. Just, "Goodbye. Had a great time." He was the perfect gentleman. Then he got back in his Caddy and drove off.

★

DEEP IN THE HEART OF TEXAS

Loni went in and listened to her phone messages, read her mail, took off her clothes, and went into the bathroom to take off her makeup. When she looked in the mirror she was smiling, grinning really. She looked at herself a long time, just grinning. She couldn't wipe that grin off her face even if she'd wanted to. Then the grin suddenly dropped and a sort of shocked look came into her eyes. That's when she realized she'd fallen for this guy.

Johnny picked Loni up for lunch the next day.

"You want to go away fishing with me?"

"I'd like to but I've got to cheer this weekend."

"Well, it doesn't have to be right away."

Then he pulled out pictures of Mexico, of his boat and Caribbean islands, natives and birds and breathtaking mountains. It was all so beautiful and fascinating.

After a few more weeks went by, Johnny asked Loni to go with him again. First, she had to go down to the nearest discount store and buy a World Atlas to find out exactly where the *Yucatan* was. Then she got to thinking about it. Fishing with a boatload of men several thousand miles from home? Maybe it wasn't such a good idea. But those photos sure looked nice. Loni didn't know what to do. . . . So she called her mother.

Loni's childhood had not been easy. Her father had been difficult to live with and both she and her mother felt a certain relief when he moved out of the country and left no forwarding address. It wasn't long before Loni's mother remarried and her step-father turned out to be even worse than her father. Loni had looked forward to being on her own and had left home as soon as she could.

"Mom this guy wants to take me on his boat through the Caribbean to the Yucatan and into Central America."

"Where's the Yucatan?"

"Mexico."

★

"Sounds like fun."

"Another thing. He's a lot older than I am. Should I go Mom?"

"Well, why not? Loni, you should never miss out on a good opportunity. The chance might never come again."

So she went. . . . And the boat turned out to be filled with men, but they couldn't wait to dock in the islands along the way so they could get at the native whores. And they had every right to think what they were probably thinking. . . . That Loni was a plaything Johnny had brought along for his and maybe even their amusement. But once they realized just how naive and innocent she really was, the men treated her fine. In fact, they even looked out for her.

The men went fishing for sailfish and drove in jeeps through some of the mountain regions hunting for jaguars. And Loni went right along with them. She'd always been a tomboy and she loved the danger and the beauty of the land. As they drove through the jungle they "went back" 2,000 years to temple ruins where natives still lived pretty much the way they had for centuries—in huts they had built.

In the heat of the day many of the natives wore almost no clothes. Their most modern convenience was a tupperware bowl and they traveled by oxen and cart. They never asked for a thing, in fact, they were always inviting these Americans into their houses and offering them food and drink.

The children were the real attraction for Loni though. She wanted to take them all home with her. They had the most innocent and open look in their eyes.

Johnny and Loni were driving back along the road one day and there was a boy standing by the side of the road with a baby parrot sitting on a stick.

"Oh, can I have it Johnny?"

★

"Of course, you can have it."

"How much for the parrot?"

"One peso."

Beyond the boy were the mountains with *piñas*—pine-apples—rising up the slopes as far as they could see. The workers with white shirts and khakis were spread out among the plants picking.

Loni gave the boy five pesos and took the bird and got back in the jeep and drove off.

It was the funniest-looking bird she'd ever seen. It was just a baby without many feathers and it had a gawky look. But he loved people. They called him "Chi Chi."

Chi Chi followed Loni around like a puppy. "Honk, honk, honk, honk!" following her every step. They took him to dinner and he walked around on the table from plate to plate, sampling the eggs and tortillas. Then he sipped the rum drinks. Oh, he loved those drinks.

At night Chi Chi would sleep on her chest right between her breasts. Just squat down and go to sleep.

Johnny left Loni on the mainland of Mexico to go on fishing expeditions. Once, after he had been gone a week, he invited her to go island hopping with him and spend an interlude together at a paradise of her choice.

Loni selected a small isle a short flight from the Yucatan. The runway there was so short, only small aircraft could fly in and out. Several planes had fallen off the end of the runway and were rusting in the ocean. The blue waters were so clear that it was possible to see the wreckage lying in a bed of coral surrounded by schools of brightly colored fish.

Only five vehicles were allowed on the island which was, ironically, about the size of a football field. In the vast ocean, it was only a speck made up of sand, palm trees, and hermit crabs in addition to the few inhabitants, who were primarily descendants of Dutch and French pirates.

★

Johnny rented a house that went for $200 a month. It was literally a single room elevated above the sand on stilts. All four walls were sliding wooden doors, one of which opened onto a bar patio. Inside were shelves lined with hundreds of books and there were also diaries left by former visitors who felt compelled to share their "dream-come-true" experiences with new arrivals.

There was no running water or electricity. Johnny and Loni had to wait for rain before they could shower. They would stand beneath a rain barrel perched on top of a two-by-four and pull a cord for a flow of water. There was no "hot" or "cold," so the trick was to soap up and be ready to rinse off quickly.

Natives were always close at hand to deal with any problems. When Loni or Johnny got thirsty, they simply asked one of the locals to climb a tree and get them a coconut.

They did all their cooking on a gas grill. One afternoon, after they had taken a small boat out to catch lobster, Johnny and Loni put water on to boil, dropped the lobster in, and snorkled around to the opposite side of the island.

They found sharks rolling around in the shallow surf, docile, they had been told, because it was mating season. Johnny and Loni waded through the unlikely scenario and took photographs.

"No one back home will even believe me," Loni thought.

It was late afternoon and the sun was beginning to set. The two strolled around the island naked, and then sat down on the sandy beach to take it all in. Not far from the edge of the sand, in the warm sea, the most spectacular show on earth was taking place. As many as two dozen dolphins surfaced and played in the rolling waves, using their fins to propel them in different directions.

It was an exciting spectacle. Johnny and Loni grasped hands in disbelief. Suddenly there were more than 100 por-

★

poises springing out of the water doing backflips and twirls. Loni and Johnny were cheering them on. The porpoises were swimming faster and leaping higher into the air.

The sun had almost set and there was an even glow, like a beachcomber's fire, throughout the islands. The neighboring isles were visible but Loni and Johnny had found the most glorious island of all. And they had witnessed one of nature's best shows. Their adrenaline rushed and their afterglow would linger for days.

Right there, in the warmth of the dying sunlight, with only amorous dolphins as witnesses, they made love.

There were no pictures or videos to show friends back home. It was just a moment in time that the two of them shared.

Finally Loni flew back to Dallas alone. Johnny had to fly to Miami on business. When she got off the plane in Dallas she was in a daze. Just last summer she was in college, and now she was in love with a man twice her age.

Totally, completely in love.

Johnny got back a week later and called and told her to put some things in a bag and come over to his place.

"Why all the clothes?"

"Oh, you're going to stay for a while."

"I am?"

"Yes."

She did as he told her, smiling the whole time. She had no idea what she was getting into, and she didn't care.

"I'll be right over," she said.

"Good. In your mailbox are some keys to a red Porsche parked out front. Drive over here in it."

"Okay. Whose is it?"

"Yours." And he hung up.

Sure enough out front was a brand new red Porsche convertible. It was the most beautiful car she'd ever seen. She

★

couldn't believe it. On the dash was a card with a red ribbon around it. She opened it and inside it read, "Beauty, start the engine and drive into my arms."

From that day on Loni was in training, although she never knew it. She moved into a bedroom that opened out onto his pool. It was a beautiful place. He had a flower garden that a Mexican gardener tended with love and she would go out in the morning and help him with the flowers. Then she'd swim and lie in the sun. She had plenty of time because she quit her job like Johnny had told her to do.

Johnny was in and out. Gone a couple of days on business trips, then back, then gone again. The house was huge and when he was home there were always a lot of people over including a lot of beautiful women. And they all loved Johnny.

One night Johnny kissed Loni and they touched each other slowly all over for a long time. She looked at him and thought what a beautiful man he was. After a while he rested her head against his thigh. . . .

She loved his voice, the way he led her. It turned her on. Whatever he wanted, she wanted. She wanted to please him. She would do anything he wanted.

"Oh, Johnny, I love you."

He just sat back watching her and giving instructions. She was a very beautiful girl. Young and eager to please. He liked that.

Finally, he laid her on the bed and for the next hour he opened her eyes to a whole new world. When they were through she was breathless, exhausted mentally and physically. She never knew making love could be so exhilarating and addictive.

They sprawled there on the bed for a while and then he leaned over and pulled a little bag out of his drawer. It was filled with white powder.

★

DEEP IN THE HEART OF TEXAS

"What's that?"

"Cocaine. Ever try it?"

"No."

"Well, I'll teach you something else then."

She did as he said and in a minute she was feeling great. They were laughing together and rolling around on the bed, making love a little and laughing.

She'd never been this happy in her life.

★

14

Suzanne had been on me about my hair for four months, all through training camp. Every day she'd say, "Do something about that damn hair!"

I was very confused about what Suzanne wanted my hair to look like. When I was growing up in Lubbock people always complimented the three of us on our long, silky, golden-blonde hair. Now I just wanted to cut it all off.

I had tried everything to please Suzanne. I had changed my hair so many times it was fried. I had gone through literally hundreds of hairdo's. I really wanted her to like me. I was always in the beautician's chair saying, "Okay, let's do something."

"How about a perm?"

"Okay. Let's try that."

Finally, one day my beautician just looked at me and said, "Your hair is falling out Stephanie. We can't do anything else with it."

I would look in the mirror for hours and cry. I hated myself.

Suzanne hated my hair because it made me look too much like Suzette. Suzette had already established her "look." She had her loyal fans who expected her to look a certain way. And Suzanne wanted me to have a different look from my sister's. She couldn't change my height or skin color or my facial features. So she focused on my hair, making my life a living hell for four months until I stumbled on the answer.

★

DEEP IN THE HEART OF TEXAS

One day I saw a long blonde ponytail attached to a hair comb and I thought, what the hell? I've tried everything else. So I bobby-pinned it to the back of my head and went to practice.

When I waltzed in, a part of me wanted to defy Suzanne and the other half of me wanted acceptance. Suzanne walked up to me and just stood there about a foot away and looked me over. Then she slowly circled me. She never changed her expression or said anything. Then finally, she said, "Will that thing stay up there while you're dancing?"

"I think so."

"Okay."

And she walked away. And that was my look. A ponytail. I'd never worn a ponytail in my life. But that was my image for the next three years and I could never change it.

I felt like a great load had been lifted from my shoulders and I could go on with my dream.

Each girl's "look" was part of the big scheme, the heart of the Cheerleaders' image. That's how Suzanne was able to plug into the fans' obsessions. She was a genius at making it work.

Each girl appealed to a certain segment of the crowd. There was the long-haired blonde, the girl with the ponytail, the pigtail girl, the tall brunette, the perky little brunette, the bouncy blonde, the sultry redhead, the freckle-faced strawberry blonde, the African-American girl, the Asian girl, the short girl, the tall girl. There was the quiet one, the sexy one, the sporty one, and the dark and mysterious one. Suzanne had one of every kind.

The fans were always checking the Cheerleaders out to see who was their favorite, who was the best-looking. The squad was made up of so many different types that just about everybody's fantasy could be fulfilled.

★

The binoculars would be focused on the Cheerleaders, "Oh, man look at those legs!"

"Yeah, but how about that face. You can't beat that face."

"Ah, I like 'em bigger in the chest."

As Suzanne got rid of one girl, she filled her spot with a look-alike. The clone of that obsession. In tryouts she would put together two girls who were similar. The best of the two would be selected. Even if both were sensational it didn't matter. She replaced girls with other girls as if she were replacing parts in a machine. Suzanne was feeding the obsession of the fans.

It's amazing that I made the squad since they already had my "look" with Suzette. After I made Cheerleader, Suzanne walked up to me and looked me square in the eye and said, "I really don't like sisters, but you were just too good to not make the squad. Don't think you made it because of Suzette. . . ." I never really knew if that was a compliment or not.

Once a girl's look had been established, she couldn't alter it one hair. I remember cutting a few wispy bangs during a brave moment. I thought I would be able to slick them back for practices and performances, but the wisps started falling down when the humidity started rising. Suzanne called me over and I knew what she was going to say.

"You're not to change your look."

"Yes ma'am."

Suzanne created images for the fans and no one had the right to change them around. Even if it was our body, we had to remain little robots, figurines crafted by Suzanne. And when any one Cheerleader left, Suzanne would find someone to fill her white boots. But Suzanne knew what she was doing. Each girl had her own faithful followers whom she turned on. Men would be yelling down, "Shake it, Stephanie! Shake it!"

★

DEEP IN THE HEART OF TEXAS

There was a family that came to every game—a husband and wife and a little boy—and they'd always stand up and yell, "We love you, Suzette," and she'd yell back to them and wave.

Fans sort of adopted us. We received dozens of presents and hundreds of pieces of fan mail every week—letters from little girls who wanted to be Cheerleaders, love letters, weird stuff, incoherent things, offers of marriage and sex and vacations with the men of our dreams.

The week after I "found my look," Suzanne called.

"Stephanie, we've chosen you for this week's "Cowboys Weekly" layout."

"Oh, Suzanne, that's fantastic! Thank you!"

"I'll be at your place on Wednesday at 3:30," and she hung up.

The Dallas Cowboys Weekly had a circulation of over 100,000 fanatical Cowboys followers. And in every issue there would be a centerfold of one of the girls. Suzanne would go to the home of the featured Cheerleader and go through her wardrobe and tell her what to wear for the photo shoot. And it was always something the girl would never pick herself, something seductive and provocative, the most revealing and sexiest clothes she could find.

The poses we were asked to strike were always overtly sexual. Sometimes the girls would be standing in a field of bluebonnets or carrying their books on campus. But some girls would be posed in lingerie sitting on a poster bed, clutching a teddy bear.

It was all part of the big tease. The closer we got to the fans, the more wholesome we were to act and dress. The farther away we got, the more sexually provocative we were made.

When Suzanne arrived at my apartment, she came right in, swept past me, and headed for my bedroom.

★

"Where's your closet?"

"My closet?"

"Yes, I'm going to pick out your clothes for your shoot."

"Well," I said, "it's back there."

Suzanne rifled through my clothes pushing the hangers to one side, inspecting this and that, ripping something off a hanger and throwing it on the bed.

"Try these on!" she ordered and she sat there and watched while I changed in and out of different outfits.

"Okay." she said, "You'll wear the sequined bikini and those blue spandex pants with the silky silver top tied up. No bra will be necessary. And then in the last shot we'll photograph you in this long yellow gown with the rhinestone belt and yellow spiked heels."

I felt a little intimidated and scared, but excited because this would be my first Cowboys Weekly layout. I was very honored and I trusted Suzanne's judgment.

The Cowboys Weekly layout epitomized, probably more than anything else, the strategy of Tex Schram, Suzanne Mitchell, and the Dallas Cowboys.

How do you tap into the paradox of the sexy, wholesome girl, the girl you'd like to take home to mother but make love to on the way over there? Well, take Miss America and dress her in hot pants and a halter top. Then put her out on a football field grinding out a lot of provocative dances, but the whole time keep telling the fans that these are good girls, wholesome girls. Barrage the fans with the girl-next-door rhetoric while you tease, tease, tease. Tell them they're not seeing what they're seeing. Make them feel like they got caught in the spin cycle of some giant brainwashing machine. Get them hot over these girls, then tell the fans they can't have them. They're sweet and untouchable. Oh, it's the stuff obsessions are forged from.

That was Schramm's genius. He recognized the power of

★

the double standard. The fact that we've never come to grips with the emotional paradox that a man can have a deep spiritual love for a woman and at the same time want to make wild love to her until, as we say in Texas, she's been rode hard and put up wet. Schramm understood America's tortured hypocrisy and tapped into its seething energy.

Schramm was very good to the press. He gave them anything they wanted because he knew that if he controlled the media, he controlled the Cowboys' image. And image, above everything else, is reality in this electronic age.

Rock Hudson's image was of the tall, dark, and handsome lover who could bed down with any girl he wanted to. Well, the truth was, he didn't want girls, he wanted boys. But that image was a reality to his fans and to the public. And Schramm was sure, more so than he was of his own name, that people would fall for whatever they were told.

He built a P.R. machine unparalleled in sports history. The Cheerleaders and their image were a very important part of his great master plan.

"I think Roger Staubach is a real-life hero," Suzanne preached. "And I honestly believe the Cheerleaders are real-life heroines to a lot of people in this country. They represent America and all that's good about it. I understand that where little girls used to dream of being Miss America, now they dream of becoming a Cheerleader for the Cowboys instead."

Schramm promoted us as the wholesome girls next door. We were a team of winners. That was the fantasy of the Cheerleaders. Tex and Suzanne manipulated and used that fantasy. They played it like a couple of business Stravinskys. That's what it was all about to them—business. And we were the merchandise!

The Cheerleaders were not Schramm's way of attracting men. He already did that with a winning team. The Cheerleaders were his way of drawing women, to get them to

★

identify with the Dallas Cowboys, with a football team. And if he had put glorified hookers out on the field, the women wouldn't have bought it. They wanted to have their *daughters* grow up to be Cheerleaders.

Of course, the Cheerleaders were bursting out of their hot pants with sexuality, but as long as they maintained the image—as long as Schramm kept telling everyone that they weren't a harem for the players or party girls for some corporate types, and that they stayed away from bars and booze—the women could accept the overflowing "C" cups and the pants cut up to Jerusalem.

Sarah Purcell interviewed Suzanne once on *Real People* and asked her the question just about everybody else asked her. "If someone were to say to you, 'Suzanne, you're selling sex here, you're really exploiting these women,' what would you say to that charge?"

"It's ridiculous!" was Suzanne's retort. "This is a voluntary thing. . . . There is nothing wrong with being sexy. That is a very beautiful quality in a woman. And especially for people to think she is a nice, clean, wholesome, sexy girl. There's nothing wrong with that. I like that. I like being sexy. Don't you?"

And Suzanne smiled the warmest, sweetest smile you ever did see. She laughed and Sarah Purcell laughed and squealed, "Woooooo!"

Suzanne was a master.

By the time Schramm was through, every little girl in Texas wanted to be a Dallas Cowboys Cheerleader and if her dream ever came true, her whole family, including Dad, was as proud as can be. Of course, Dad was the same guy who had sat with his buddies in a bar sloshing down brewskies and watching the football game on Sunday afternoon. He fantasized, "Oh, baby, do it to me!" when the camera flashed to the Cheerleaders—the bare midriff, the long gor-

★

geous legs, the belly buttons, the overflowing boobs, the lipstick and the hair. Yes, that was dear old Dad until the day his darling daughter became a Cheerleader. Then all those girls were just nice, wholesome girls for whom sex meant nothing.

In early 1979, Dallas Cowboys Cheerleaders, Inc., was the plaintiff in a court case against Pussycat Cinema in New York. The bone of contention was that *Debbie Does Dallas*, an X-rated film, was made to take advantage of what most of the male population was already fantasizing about.

After several rounds of injunctions and plenty of legal maneuvering, the showing of the movie at the Pussycat was ultimately cancelled. DCC Inc. had won its case based on the unauthorized infringement of the trademark name and uniform. It seems Debbie was "doing" Dallas dressed in a uniform altogether too similar to that of the Dallas Cowboys Cheerleaders.

Suzanne spent enormous amounts of time and money restraining the movie throughout the country. She also managed to have the offending uniforms omitted from the film.

Oh, we all cheered when we heard that we had won. Way to go, DCC Inc.! Beating the pornographers. Our parent organization had gone out and smitten the fire-breathing dragon. DCC Inc. had ventured into his very lair, called him out, and challenged him.

But the irony of the whole thing was that Tex and Suzanne had created that monster. They'd nurtured and fed it until it grew scales and fangs and they'd fueled its lust until this pornographic monster emerged from our collective libido.

Debbie Does Dallas was the filmed fantasy of every American man's daydream. Every Sunday after church there was a whole stadium full of private viewings of *Debbie Does Dallas* going on in the fecund mind of the male fan with his

★

binocs zoomed in on those luscious bazooms. "Oh, baby!" he'd groan, and that tape playing in his head would make "Debbie" seem like "Mary Poppins."

And that was sometimes a problem. If you keep pushing the fantasy button you can get more than you bargained for—namely, an obsession. There were a few fans out there on the lunatic fringe who would focus on a Cheerleader and never let go. The fan's whole life would become fixated on one Cheerleader. He'd collect any picture of her that he could get his hands on and send them all to her to autograph.

Wholesome or not, we were meant to be sexy. We were doing provocative dances, and it drove some fans nuts. We were setting the weird personalities up and getting set up ourselves.

Some of these nuts knew the girl's name and would go looking for her all over the stadium. They didn't even stop at the gates. Every girl had some guy calling her, pursuing her . . . driving her crazy. Some were the kind to turn sexually threatening and violent.

At the end of every quarter of the game each group of girls moved to a different corner of the field. One guy would follow me from corner to corner in the stadium. He had a poster with my picture on it and my name printed underneath, STEPHANIE. And he held it up every time I'd look anywhere near his direction.

After the game, sure enough, he'd be out in the parking lot, waiting.

"Stephanie! Stephanie! Did you see me waving at you in the stands?"

"Oh, yes. I saw you." You try your best to be nice to these pathetic people and hope it doesn't escalate into an obsession. But the signs are all there. And they aren't good.

"Here are the pictures I took during the game of you. Do you like this one? This is my favorite shot." Or "I like the

★

way you moved during that number in the third quarter."

He knew my whole life story too. He knew I was from Lubbock, that I'd been a cheerleader at MacKenzie Junior High and Coronado High School, everything. And all I could think was, "Get the hell out of my life." All with a smile on my face, of course.

Then, somehow, although we always had our phone numbers unlisted, he got mine. And that's when the nightmare began.

"Stephanie," he'd whisper and get me out of a deep sleep at three or four in the morning.

"Yes?"

And he'd start in with the foul, spooky stuff.

"Please, please, stop calling me," I pleaded. "If you really like me as you say you do, you wouldn't torture me like this. You're really hurting me. I'm getting the police after you."

"How are you gonna prove it's me."

I immediately called the police but the calls kept coming for six months. "I know when you're home. Don't you think I don't. One of these days you're gonna be alone and I'm gonna get you."

I was constantly looking out the window to see if there was a strange car parked out front. I was petrified, a prisoner in my own apartment. I would change phone numbers and it would stop for a while, but then the phone would ring one night.

"Stephanie?"

"Yes."

"Stephanie. This is your lover. I can't get my mind off of you."

And he'd start in again.

I finally lost him when I got married and moved twice in three weeks.

Some girls had it worse than I did. *Katy Ferris* got a

★

package with knives in it and a letter explaining in detail exactly what was going to be done with those knives.

One day she was taking a nap in the bedroom of her apartment and she woke up to a man standing there looking at her. When she moved, he just turned and slipped out the sliding glass door.

For two years a weirdo followed *Marta Vance* around. He even followed her to work. There had been several rapes in her building so she was really afraid. She had a long walk to her car and she'd see him waiting for her.

At the games he tried to give her presents and in the beginning she took them. Then it got serious. She would have her roommate on one side and her boyfriend on the other, plus a security guard. They'd meet her right at the entrance to the tunnel where she emerged after the game. This guy would be right on her, leaning over them to get at her, talking to her the whole time they walked to her car.

Eventually, he found out where she lived. That's when the nature of the cards and letters he'd been sending changed. Before he had to send them through the Cowboys front office. Now he could send them directly to her. The ones she would get through Suzanne were always nice and sweet. But the ones he began sending to her house told her in the grossest of detail exactly what he was going to do to her.

The police told Marta that they couldn't do a thing until he actually attacked her though.

It got even worse. After the Super Bowl in 1978 we were riding back on the plane with the media. Somehow, this guy got a pass and got on board the plane. Marta was asleep and he slipped into the seat next to her and sat there and watched her for three hours while she slept.

When we were getting off the plane, KVIL personality Ron Chapman was right behind Marta and this guy wouldn't

★

leave her alone. He kept trying to shove a present in her hand.

"Take it Marta, please."

"No. Look, I don't want any more presents. I don't want anything from you."

Marta got rough with him. She'd had it. She was scared and frustrated. She just wanted him to go away.

"Just go back into the hole you crawled out of and leave me alone!"

When they got down to the bottom of the stairs of the plane, he threw the present on the tarmac and began to stomp on it and scream. He was screaming at the top of his voice. But really *screaming* like a woman would scream, a high-pitched wail like a wild animal. Just screaming like a child having a tantrum.

Ron was stunned. He stood there in shock because, like everyone else, he thought of our lives as idyllic, just bouncy little girls without a care in the world. Ron was shaking too. He walked Marta out to her car to make sure she made it home okay.

Finally, Marta reached her breaking point, so she called her boyfriend's father. He has a deep, gruff voice that can scare the britches off a mule. He found out where this guy worked and called him at his job and told him, "If you ever contact Marta again, I'll kill you, boy. I know where you live and I'll come over there and get you. Don't ever call her. Don't ever write her. Don't ever try to see her any time, any place or you're a dead man."

Marta never heard from her weirdo again.

★

15

When a girl was a Dallas Cowboys Cheerleader she became obsessed with how she looked. From the first day we joined the squad it was drummed into us by Suzanne that we represented the Dallas Cowboys and all of Texas and even America. Therefore, we had an obligation to look perfect all the time. Not just at games or personal appearances. All the time. We weren't even allowed to go to the grocery store without our makeup and hair in place. One girl went to a Tom Thumb store in her curlers and wouldn't you know, Suzanne just happened to be at that store shopping too. Every time one of us did something wrong, there she was.

Eventually, we were all snared by the same things that trap every other American woman: The quest for perfection in her looks. The only difference between us and all those other women was that we were under a microscope. Just think . . . we had all the neuroses of the American woman magnified a thousand times. Our egos, however, were as frail as the frumpiest housewife's.

Eileen Ford, who owns the largest modeling agency in New York, described the ideal model. Over five ten, big wide-set eyes, straight nose, generous lips, and a long neck. But how many girls are 5'10" to start with and have lips like Julia Roberts? American women try to hammer, reshape, and medically alter themselves into this idea. Everybody's trying to look like the cover of *Cosmo*. Only the girls on the

★

cover of *Cosmo* don't even look that good. A lot of it is airbrushing, lighting, makeup, and oftentimes plastic surgery.

Suzanne demanded that we strive for the perfect figure. That was the root of our problem. That perfect figure that you see in *Vogue* today rarely exists—a tiny, tiny rear end with a tiny waist and big breasts. That's not a body you see a lot in nature, it's a manufactured body. Our ideal in America today can seldom be found. We're trying to attain a perfection that takes superior genes, an anorexic mentality, a fantastic exercise regimen, and in many cases, plastic surgery. Only one or two girls on the squad had a naturally perfect figure, and they had to starve themselves to maintain it.

This national quest to achieve physical perfection is poisoning the happiness of American women. This idea that a woman can never be too thin or too beautiful, this constant self-scrutiny to always look better, can really destroy confidence and self-esteem simply because attaining perfection is impossible.

I remember *Gloria Smith* telling me how the experience affected her.

"Before I made Cheerleader," she said, "I couldn't have told you what I weighed. I was okay. It didn't make that much difference exactly what I weighed. As a result, I really always felt pretty good about myself. Then when I made Cheerleader, the uniform and the pressure to be a certain weight played tricks with my mind. You'd think it would be the most confident time of my life. But I was a wreck. I had no confidence at all. I thought I was fat and ugly.

"Finally, my father said, 'Gloria, your values are changing. You're becoming too aware of what you look like and not who you are.'

"He was right. I was becoming a Dallas Cowboys Cheer-

★

leader all the time. It wasn't just the games or personal appearances any more. It was becoming a part of my life every single second to where I no longer thought that being Gloria was good enough. I had to be Gloria, the Dallas Cowboys Cheerleader with the great hair and the great legs . . . the perfect weight, weighing about 100 pounds."

I remember asking Careene at the campout, "How do you stop from getting a big head about all this?"

"Oh, just wait until the first practice," she laughed.

At the first practice Suzanne called us one by one into her office for an inspection. Without any eye contact she walked up to each girl and scrutinized her from head to toe, looking at each body like it was secondhand merchandise at a swap meet. Then she'd write something in the little black notebook that she always carried.

As she went along Suzanne would also tell each girl what she didn't like about her. . . . This one had to change the color of her hair. That one had to cut hers. The next girl had to do something about those nails. "Get a manicure and then we'll go from there," Suzanne would snap. "Nails are the fine point of a lady."

Suzanne was toughest when it came to our weight. She thought most of the girls had to lose a few pounds. After that first practice she handed out these thick, black ring binders that contained the rules and regulations and what was expected of us. Then on the very last page she had a weight chart and a listing of ten different areas in which girls might have to lose weight—thighs, hips, waist, arms, and so on. Some of the girls were marked in every category.

"Start now by losing those extra pounds," Suzanne told us. "The camera adds ten pounds to your frame and those uniforms are smaller than you think. Every ripple or bulge will show. You have to earn the right to wear one of those uniforms. It's as recognizable as the American flag and I will

★

not let you disgrace it. Unless I see you continually at your best, you'll be put on probation for one game, and then cut if the problem is not resolved. Period."

When some of the girls were told to lose weight, they were in shock. They had always been in great shape. Most of them had danced all their lives and just never considered weight a problem. They'd always been tiny. No one had ever said they were overweight before.

None of us ever considered that Suzanne could be wrong, however. So we all immediately went on diets. All we knew was that we were flawed and, like the overachievers we were, we set out to fix ourselves.

Suzanne had told one girl to lose twenty pounds before the first cut. So when the practice broke up, she ran around to the veterans and asked, "When's the first cut?"

"Three weeks," Zee said.

"Three weeks! I can't lose twenty pounds in three weeks. I'd have to stop eating completely. How could I dance?"

"Welcome to the wonderful world of diet pills."

Later that year when we starred in a *Love Boat* episode, I was sitting with the man who plays Isaac, the black bartender on the show. He said to me, "You are 36 of the most beautiful girls in the world and you're all down on yourselves. It doesn't make any sense. You're all beautiful, talented, and everybody loves you. Who'd believe it? Something is wrong. Something is tearing you apart. You're all too beautiful to be feeling this way about yourselves."

I looked at him and I didn't understand a word he was saying.

Suzanne herself was thin. She was as thin as the cigarettes she smoked. She looked at fat like a Baptist preacher looks at sex. It was evil. So there was constant pressure on us to stay scary-thin. If you were scary-thin, Suzanne liked you. The emphasis on an anorexic body was so high, the praise

★

was heaped so heavily on us when we were in that emaciated condition, that we all wanted to look that way. We were conditioned to think that starvation was good and food was bad.

Suzanne was obsessed with fat. On Monday we would have a weigh-in. We had to be whatever weight she thought we should be. Health, periodic bloat, ideal weight—those things were never considered. She picked a number out and we had to be that weight.

Suzanne chain-smoked Virginia Slims and drank iced coffee all day long. When the sun went down she'd switch to hot coffee, so she was wired tighter than a suitcase bomb—ready to explode at any minute.

At practice or before a game, she'd walk around like a drill sergeant inspecting her troops. One day she walked up behind *Joy Noroozi*, a beautiful blonde with a figure like Madonna, and grabbed a fistful of her butt. With a "this is the most vile stuff I've ever seen" look on her face, Suzanne spit out the words "lose weight!" Her command hung in the room like the drops of venom left hanging on the fangs of a rattler after it strikes.

Gail Gibson was one of the girls on the team whom this obsession affected the most.

Gail looked like a movie star. She would get stopped all the time by people on the street asking for her autograph. After she signed her name, they'd say, "A Cheerleader! Wow! I thought you were just an actress. This is great!"

Suzanne pressured Gail about her weight. Any girl on the street would have commited a felony to have a figure like Gail's, but as a Cheerleader she was considered fat.

One evening, I was supposed to pick Gail up on the way to practice. I honked the horn out front but when she didn't come out right away, I went to her apartment and knocked. Gail came to the door in a panic.

"Oh, Stephanie," she screamed, "I can't find my diet pills."

★

And she ran back into her bedroom. The place was a shambles. The couch was torn apart, the cushions thrown here and there around the room, and the cabinets and drawers were all open.

"Gail, we're going to be late."

I went into her bedroom after her and she was tossing shoes out of her closet, pulling sweaters and things off the shelves.

"Gail? What are you doing? We've gotta go!"

"I've got to find those pills. I can't make it through practice without them."

"If we miss this practice, she won't let us cheer."

"I know. Oh, God." And she started crying. "We've got the weigh-in today and Suzanne said if I didn't lose five pounds this week I would be sitting in the dressing room for this week's game."

"How about your water weight?"

"I took fiber pills and a diuretic last night and I haven't had anything to drink all day."

"Did you run?"

"Six miles this morning."

"And?"

"I'm at 103 right on the nose." Gail was 5′6″, so she was actually about 15 pounds under ideal weight.

"What's the problem then?"

"I'm exhausted Stephanie. I haven't eaten all week. I've just had these black mollies. I know I can't make it. But if I don't make it through practice, I won't cheer. No matter what the problem is. So I will have gone through all this for nothing. I just can't make it!" And she sat down on the floor in the middle of her bedroom with her clothes and shoes and books strewn everywhere and sobbed.

"I just can't make it!," she kept saying over and over.

One of the side effects of amphetamines is that they ex-

★

aggerate moods and tension. We didn't need any more help in that area since we were already under so much pressure.

I grabbed Gail by her arm and led her out the door and into my car.

"Take a deep breath. Close your eyes. Focus all your energy on relaxing. I'll help you make it through practice."

Gail wasn't alone in her obsession. Girls did drastic things on a daily basis to lose weight. *Nanci Edwards* put cellulite cream on her thighs, wrapped them in cellophane and wore pantyhose over that. Then she put a heating pad on the offending area and went to bed. When she woke up she had blisters all over her bottom.

Many of the girls wore heavy rubber pants to practice everyday to sweat the pounds off. They'd take them off after practice and they'd be full of water. To compound this folly, Suzanne would seldom permit us to drink water or to put on the air conditioner. This was to acclimate us to the heat of Texas Stadium in the summer. It was pure madness. Girls sometimes passed out at practice and charley horses were common because we didn't have enough fluids in our systems to prevent cramping.

The Scholtz sisters were not immune to the insanity. Suzette went over to Korea on a USO tour and came back home with a terrible bug. She was in the hospital for a few days and sick as a dog for weeks. But she was happy because she was losing weight.

When she came back, Suzanne brought her up in front of everyone and said, "Ladies, take a good look at Suzette. That's the way we want you to look."

"Yeah," Lisa whispered, "and all you have to do is get hospitalized to look that way."

Chris Stone carried a little sack of pills with her everywhere. It was filled with laxatives, dexies, black mollies, and sleeping pills. She would never go to dinner with us because

★

she knew she'd break down and eat and she didn't want to eat. Chris never ate. She'd just take her pills.

Cindy Bacon was another one. She was a beautiful brunette who dieted and took so many diuretics that she lost her hearing for a while. As a matter of fact, she nearly lost it permanently. She finally went to a doctor and he scolded her, "What do you think you're doing? You've drained all the fluids from your body and your ears have dried out. You have no hearing left. If you don't stop taking these diuretics and diet pills, you're going to be permanently deaf."

When she came to practice the next day, Cindy was crying her eyes out.

"I don't know how else to lose weight. And if I don't lose this weight, Suzanne'll throw me off the team."

"You don't have an ounce of fat left on you, Cindy."

"Suzanne said I need to lose five more pounds. I'm taking diet pills. I'm not eating anything. I just can't lose weight without diuretics. I just can't do it."

DeeDee was another girl with a serious health problem that almost killed her. She was always in the bathroom throwing up. We thought she was on drugs or she was nervous or something. She went through three years of throwing up. Then she went to the doctor and he rushed her into the hospital and removed her thyroid. He told her she should have been dead.

Several of the Cheerleaders were true bulemics. They would throw up all night long, and then eat candy bars and cookies and go in and throw up again. They wanted to eat but couldn't stand the guilt when they did, so they'd get rid of it.

To compound this madness about our weight, our schedules were ridiculous. We went to work or school all day and then we danced full out at practice every evening. Drugs and stimulants were a necessity. I lived on donuts and reg-

★

ularly drank 10 to 12 cups of coffee a day stiffened with spoonfuls of sugar. Many of the girls took diet pills for the weigh-in, for practice, for the game, and to stay up to study. We all got caught up in the frenzy in one way or another. After practice, at one or two in the morning, we'd all go down to the local all-night eateries and gorge on high calorie junk like banana splits and greasy french fries dipped in mayonnaise. Then, we'd fast for two days.

Most of us used diuretics to make weigh-in. We'd take them twenty-four hours before weigh-in in order to drop our water weight. This was hard on our bodies to begin with. But considering that we had to dance for five grueling hours in a steaming hot room after an overdose of diuretics, it was *very* hard on our bodies. But that's what we did. We'd show up Monday morning dehydrated like prunes, but we always made weight.

Everything was in excess. We ate too much. We drank too much. We practiced too much. And we never slept. Yet we were expected to be on every night, dance full-throttle, and never miss a beat. And the next morning we had to get up and go to school. Then it was back to practice. On our off days, about once every two or three weeks, we pulled the plug on the phone and slept all day and all night.

We followed this nightmarish regimen in order to be a Dallas Cowboys Cheerleader. It was very important, a dream realized. The only problem was trying to live that dream. And with the workaholic schedule, Suzanne driving us, and the hysterical roller coaster of highs and degradations that was nearly impossible.

In the end, a few of the girls found the best answer was stronger and stronger drugs. That inevitably meant cocaine, the Cadillac of speed. The girls who were the heaviest into cocaine were among the thinnest girls on the squad. Their ribs and hipbones showed through their skin, and their

★

cheeks were sunk into their faces. They looked the best in the uniform though, because it fit in such a way that unless we were skin and bones, we always looked a little fat in it. These were the girls that were brought up in front of the group and praised.

Everybody knew who was snorting cocaine because they were so skinny. Nobody could dance that much and lose weight. Fuel was needed for all that exercise. It's not possible to be that emaciated and still work that hard. Without "the little helper" they just didn't have enough energy.

Food was the enemy.

Cooki Simms bragged that her secret to losing weight was cocaine and raisins.

"A raisin and cocaine diet! What are the raisins for?" Zee asked her.

"Fiber."

"Well, I'm glad to see you're not neglecting your health."

Cocaine and the Dallas Cowboys Cheerleaders were a devilish little serendipity that happens sometimes in life. Coke came onto the popular scene just about the same time as the Cheerleaders hit it big. And it was a perfect little marriage of convenience for some of the girls.

And where were these Dallas Cowboys Cheerleaders getting all of their coke from? Why, from the Cocaine Cowboy, Johnny Robinson.

★

ohnny Robinson's fishing and hunting expeditions covered up his drug smuggling. Loni didn't know all this yet. All she knew was he had more money than she thought possible and they always had plenty of coke around the house for partying.

One night Johnny came in very late and woke Loni up.

"Beauty! Help me count this money!" he said.

"What time is it?"

"I don't know. Three, four in the morning. Wake up!"

Johnny dumped a trash bag filled with money on the living room floor. They spent two hours separating ones, fives, tens, twenties, fifties, and hundred dollar bills.

"Johnny, where did you get all this money?"

"My restaurants."

"My God! They must be doing great!"

"Easiest money I ever made."

For the next hour they counted money.

"$289,433!"

"I never thought I'd see this much money in my life, much less be sitting in the middle of it."

"Here," he said and tossed her a couple of bundles. "Go buy a new dress."

"That's $10,000!"

"So buy an expensive dress."

One night, Loni and Cooki were out dancing and Cooki pulled out a joint.

★

"Have you ever smoked dope?"

"A couple of times in college."

"Do you want to smoke this?"

"Why not?"

They had a blast that night. Two crazy girls drinking and dancing and flirting with everyone. It was nothing but fun.

Then one day Cooki showed up at Loni's house with a surprise in her purse.

"Wanna try some coke?"

And she pulled out this little vial of white powder. So Loni went over to the closet and reached in and pulled out a rock of cocaine the size of a football and laid it in front of Cooki.

Cooki lit up like a new saloon.

One day Cooki was over snorting coke when Johnny came home.

"Hi, honey. I want you to meet Cooki."

"Hi, Cooki."

"Cooki's another Cheerleader."

"Oh, another Cheerleader."

And that's when the game changed. Johnny had a new source of power. He had a whole harem of Cheerleaders. Not for himself so much but for his "friends."

Johnny treated Loni's friends like queens. They knew that they could come over any time they wanted and snort all the cocaine they wanted and take home lots of free samples.

What Johnny got in return was their loyalty. There were three to five regulars from the squad who showed up at his place. And Johnny was the master of ceremonies. It was a show every night. He had the friendship of the most coveted stable of women in Dallas—the Cowboys Cheerleaders. But more importantly, he knew the Cheerleaders who loved to party. All a man had to do was know Johnny Robinson and

★

he could be at those parties. And the next thing he knew, he'd probably have a Cheerleader on his arm and be the envy of every man in Texas.

Coke was just becoming popular then and supposedly it wasn't addictive. It didn't make people act foolish or sloppy. It woke them up. It made them feel like partying. It made them feel like dancing. There wasn't any crack cocaine around and most people didn't freebase. Just snort a little, get high a little. And, bingo! Party time. It seemed harmless enough. It was the perfect drug.

Coke was part of the glamour of the Dallas boom. Guys would pull out a thousand dollar bill, roll it tight and snort a line. And, of course, the reason for the big bill was that "you get a lot higher if you do it with a thousand dollar bill, trust me, honey."

Coke was a social drug, something you did like having a glass of wine. It was part of the social scene. Of course it was still illegal. Everyone made sure they didn't get caught. But socially it was acceptable. In fact, it was expected.

The Cheerleaders who used cocaine would go out to dinner at an expensive restaurant, order a ton of food—appetizers, entrée upon entrée, wine, dessert. Somebody would always have some coke and they'd go in pairs to the ladies room and get high. In no time they were too high to eat. So they'd get up and leave with a table full of food in front of them and go to Elan's and dance all night.

The parties Johnny Robinson threw became legend around Dallas. And Loni was the hostess. The Cocaine Cowboy and the Cowboys Cheerleader. It could have been a movie.

Johnny already felt like a king before he met Loni. She was just an extra bauble. But oh how she made the whole picture sparkle! She added that brilliant spotlight to his

★

whole party. She was the celebrity that legitimized what he was doing.

"Oh, baby, I saw you on TV today!"

"How many times?"

"Seven."

"All right!"

When Loni started bringing home her Cheerleader friends, Johnny's ego rush was pushed up another notch.

One night Lisa and Kim and Cooki all went to Johnny and Loni's house for a big party.

When they pulled up to his estate, Johnny and Loni greeted them at the door.

"Hi! Come on in. It's cold out there."

He led them through a door and there were two long narrow tables set up in the middle of the room. On the tables were the names of every guest spelled out in cocaine.

"Here," he said and handed them each a hundred dollar bill. "Before you can start partying, you've got to snort up your name."

"I'm glad I've got a short name," Lisa laughed.

"Oh, don't worry! I took care of that. The short names are written in the big script."

Sure enough, there were Lisa and Cooki and Kim emblazoned across one of the tables.

Johnny had covered the tables in light blue paper and spelled the names out in the white powder, so it looked like a skywriter had flown around and had written their names in white smoke. He even had "clouds" of cocaine here and there to complete the picture.

"Yeah, you can stop off at one of those extra little piles if you really want to get on Cloud 9."

*   *   *

★

Loni and Johnny were making out in the jacuzzi, oblivious to the people splashing around them.

"Who cares?" Loni thought.

"That's the feeling you get when you're snorting all that coke—who cares? All you want to know is, What are we going to do next for fun?"

★

17

Suzette, Sheri, and I were lucky. We didn't use drugs or get hooked on them. Thanks, once again, to our upbringing and the constant vigilance of our parents. Mother and Daddy paid close attention to who we associated with and they preached to us about drugs and alcohol from the time we started school.

Even Mamie warned us constantly about the dangers of drugs. She'd sit us down and tell us stories about what drugs could do to us. And it was all first-hand stuff because she'd done her share of drinking in her day.

Years back, I joined AA. I realized I was drinking too much. Oh, I'm a party girl! All my life I loved to party. I'm 70 now, I'm still a party girl. I love a good time. I love to be around happy people.

The first time I went to AA was with my cousin Leo. They handed out a little test of twenty-five questions. I remember that it said, "Answer the questions. AND TELL THE TRUTH!"

The questions were all in regard to your drinking habits and how they affected you. So I filled it out and handed it back to Leo and said, "Well, I just scored a 100 on that one. I'm in trouble. I think I'm gonna join y'all.

If anybody hollered 'party' I was there. I'd usually get carried away and drink too much. Told all the family secrets. Didn't eat properly. Drank on an empty stomach and

★

called it dinner. Thank God I never got to the blackout stage. Why, some of those people would get on a plane and they'd wake up in another city and have no idea what happened.

Most women are protected because they drink at home. I didn't. I drank all over. One drink and I was off and running. I didn't hide out. But most ladies do. By the time the husband gets home, she's bombed.

I had a sister-in-law who was a bad one. M.D.'s wife, Eloise. How he stayed with her I don't know. She kept getting drunk earlier and earlier in the day. After awhile she was drunk 24 hours a day. And it wasn't just booze either. She was on all kinds of pills too. She popped those Miltowns like they were popcorn. She had a jar in her kitchen big as Aunt Jemima, filled with different colored pills. No tellin' how many a day she'd take.

Anyway, M.D. died and his funeral was the worst experience I've ever been through in my entire life. He was in San Diego and we knew he was gonna die any day. So Sue and I drove out there together. Eloise was living in their mobile home. Dump ain't no word for it. And dirty!

She had on a pants suit. And it was a good one too. But she'd been wearing it no telling how long.

She'd go to sleep on the divan and wet herself. Days and days like this. The divan was soaked. I'm talking about filth. I don't have a keen smeller but she still smelled like a wet goat.

"We've got to get that nasty place of hers cleaned up," I told Sue. "The relatives and friends will be showin' up. I don't want M.D. embarrassed. I don't know how we're gonna get her clean. She's gonna need a corn cob and Dutch Cleanser."

Sue and I cleaned that filthy place up. I told Sue, "I want every dish, everything that isn't nailed down washed.

★

I don't want any part of her filth on anything I touch. Load the dishwasher, unload it, and load it again."

She had an afghan on the divan that she'd been wettin' and dryin', wettin' and dryin'. It was a beautiful thing her mother had made.

"What are you gonna do with this?" Sue asked.

"Wash it!"

"Why, it'll shrink."

"I don't care if it shrinks down to where it wouldn't cover a baby."

Anyway, they called us from the hospital at the hotel we were staying in to tell us M.D. had died. So we went over to Eloise's trailer to tell her he'd passed away. She was drunk, of course.

She had an old flea-bitten wig that was as filthy as she was. Well, she socked it on. It sat up there crooked on her head. And, of course, she had on the same old pants suit. My God, she looked like the "Grapes of Wrath."

We took her, got a wheelchair, and pushed her into the hospital. The doctor came out, told us what happened and that they would like to have an autopsy taken on M.D. to see what had really happened.

Well, Eloise had a fit right there in the hospital. "Nobody's gonna cut on my baby! Nobody's cuttin' my baby!"

All that kind of crap. Rolling around and screamin' and moanin'.

We got her out of there finally. So on the way back I told Eloise, "You're a selfish person. If they do an autopsy on M.D. it might save a life next time around."

Finally she said, "Oh, just call 'em and tell 'em they can do the autopsy."

They were delighted, of course.

So that was a good excuse for Eloise to get really drunk and from then on she pointed her finger at me.

★

"Ohhhhhh," and she'd start bawling. "You're the one that did it. You're the one that let them cut my baby!"

Sue and I took care of all the details. We took Eloise down to the funeral parlor to select the casket. Same scene. Smelling like you know what. Drunk as two Marines. Well, we walked in the place and Sue and I went in with Eloise right behind. Only when we get in the door, we make a right and Eloise makes a left. She starts heading down to where they were preparing for another service with the casket all set up and everything.

Well, Eloise saw that casket and she was on a downhill pull right for it. I saw what she was doing and started running after her.

"Eloise! Eloise! That's not him! That's not him!"

I caught her just as she got to the casket and was leaning down to give this poor old soul a big wet 100 proof kiss. The friends of the deceased were appalled. What was this drunk stranger doing kissing our Wally?

Finally, I steered her back out and she kept hollering, "My baby! My baby!"

I got her in where they show you the caskets they got and right away, of course, she's shootin' for the most expensive one. "Forget the deluxe model with the feather pillow, Eloise," I told her. "M.D. was a plain man, he'll be happy with a plain coffin."

It got worse at the funeral. When the minister started reading from the scripture, he'd get about three words out and Eloise would hollar, "Ahhhhhhhh, crap!"

The minister would raise his voice a little and keep going.

"Ahhhhhhhhhh, crap!" This went on for a while then the minister cut the service short.

Poor M.D. He was probably doing somersaults in that box of his.

★

DEEP IN THE HEART OF TEXAS

When we sold our house in Tucson, Joe left me to sell it. This was before I joined AA. So, anyway, I had an open house. My cousin-uncle M.I. came to help me. He was Grandma Valentine's boy, a miner, worked down in those holes for years and years. He's dead now. Great guy. Anyway, he came out to help me unload this house and we had a hell of a time selling it. It was a General Motors executive's house. We'd bought it furnished. What a place! You name it, it had it. Lord, it had purple carpeting in the living room. It was a whore's nightmare.

Anyway, this couple came by about five in the afternoon. I said to M.I., "We might have a bite here."

"Maybe so."

They were older people, you could tell they had money and they really liked the place. Shows you can't buy taste.

When they came in M.I. said, "Would you like to have a cocktail?"

The old man turned it down but boy I mean she jumped at it. "Yes, I believe I would."

I slipped back into the kitchen to fix the drinks and I thought I'd give her a double shot to help make her mind up. I eased on back out. She threw that one down like lemonade. So I jumped right on her.

"Would you like another one?"

"Why sure."

So back into the kitchen and, oooops, another double deal. One right after another. The old man tried to slow her down. I don't know how many she had but awhile later she had to go to the bathroom. I showed her down the hall and came back and all of a sudden I heard a big plop! So I ran down the hall.

Now the way they were talking I knew they were very interested in buying the house. By then they'd made an

★

appointment to meet me for breakfast the next morning to talk over the deal.

Anyway, I went to the bathroom and she was on the floor, passed out drunk. She was a big woman. A great big fatty. All girdled out. It was like a big bucket of blubber spilled out on the floor.

I wrestled with her all by myself because I couldn't ask for any help, of course. Finally, I rassled those panties on and got that girdle back up by shaking her in it, one side to the other. Then I got her out of the bathroom and down the hall and sat her down.

The old man looked at her and he wanted to kill us both.

When he got her into the car and took off, I looked over to M.I. and said, "Well, wave good-bye to the only decent bite we've had all month."

Sure enough he called later that afternoon.

"I'm going to have to cancel that breakfast appointment. My wife will be hung over in the morning."

I felt sorry for the old boy. He had a handful there. She was an alcoholic. That's the reason she got drunk so fast. She'd been sippin' when he wasn't looking. She was loaded before she got there. And you can bet she had a bottle in her pocket.

Oh, I tell you that booze and drugs can destroy a life quicker than two tornadoes.

★

18

The glamour and excitement of being a Dallas Cowboys Cheerleader, as portrayed by the media in magazines, on TV, and in movies, is how most people perceived us. But there was a lot more to the Cheerleaders then the glamour.

Probably, the greatest thing Suzanne Mitchell ever did as director of the Cheerleaders was to let us to bring joy to those less fortunate—to orphans and the handicapped, and to our lonely servicemen stationed in far-off lands.

By far, the most rewarding of the personal appearances were the charity events. The memories almost every Cheerleader cherishes the most were of our trips to hospitals and orphanages, and our USO tours visiting our troops throughout the world. It made us feel special, like we were really doing something worthwhile, really helping other people.

On Saturdays, or on the Sundays when the Cowboys were playing out of town, we usually visited rest homes, VA hospitals, and orphanages. And we almost always went away with a great feeling.

On one visit, Suzette sat down next to an old man in a VA mental ward. He just sat there rocking . . . rocking and grinding his teeth. He never talked or even looked at her.

"You know," she told him, "there's really someone out there who cares about you. I hope you have a great Christmas."

Then she signed a picture for him and as she got up he

★

put a steel grip on her wrist. Her heart started palpitating. He never looked at her but out of the corner of his mouth he said, "Nobody ever told me they cared before." Then he slowly released his grip. Suzette walked slowly out of that hospital with tears streaming down her face.

The orphanages we visited were always the most moving experience for us. Once a year we visited the Buckner Baptist Children's Home in Dallas. We'd go in and do a performance for the kids in the cafeteria. Then we'd eat with them and go up to the girls' dorm and see where they lived. Mostly though, we just talked and signed autographs for several hours. And these kids just hung on our every word, clinging to our arms, looking up at us in awe.

There was one family of kids I got to know—two older boys, six and eight, and a little girl of three. A family was going to only adopt the little girl and the children didn't know what to do.

"Nobody wants Bobby and me," Brian, the oldest boy said, "because we're too old. But they'll take Christy because she's only three. We know it's impossible for a family to take all three of us. The orphanage is trying to keep us all together but it doesn't look like they're going to be able to." At eight, Bobby was the head of the family. After talking about it he decided Christy should go. "At least she'll have a home."

Leaving that day broke all our hearts. In front of the Buckner Home is a large expanse of grass, an acre or more in size. When we left the kids followed us out to our bus. We boarded and were waving good-bye and as we went out through the gates the attendants closed them behind us and the kids pressed up against the wrought iron bars of the fence. Then our bus turned and went down the street and the kids started chasing us across the huge grassland in front of the orphanage—running for all they were worth until they came to the far edge of the yard and they couldn't run any

★

farther. Then they stuck their hands through the bars as if they were trying to grab the bus and hold us there just a little while longer.

Rarely did the entire squad travel together. Instead, Suzanne and Texie put together a Show Group of eight to twelve of the most talented, most beautiful girls to represent the squad. We had to do something besides show up and do some pom-pom numbers so Texie put together a traveling variety show.

The William Morris Agency represented and sold us to fans across the country. We performed at State Fairs, conventions, and halftime shows from coast to coast and around the world. The Show Group wasn't a cheerleading squad. It was a troupe of very talented dancers, singers, gymnasts, and ballerinas.

During the hour that we performed we became quick-change artists as we entered and exited the stage to complete ten musical numbers with eight costume changes. We began shedding our clothes as soon as we reached the curtain off stage. Tap and ballet shoes would fly, and zippers and buttons were rarely fastened until seconds before stepping onto the stage. There was no time to breathe between numbers. If any piece to any costume was left back in Dallas, the girl was sent home with no questions asked. We double- and triple-checked our luggage before getting on the airplane and before each performance. No one took any chances.

Our show always opened with our hit number, "We Love the Cowboys." Suzette would then flip and tumble across the stage as Dolores and *Mary Beth* would appear, surprising the crowd with a ballet number. The pace of the show was picked up again by Lisa and Careene who would entertain the audience with a musical comedy. An electrifying *Fame* dance number by several girls followed and then while everyone changed costumes, Inger melted the audience with her

★

singing and guitar strumming. Clad in our famous blue and white uniforms, we would bring the show to a rousing end with our dance and kickline rendition of . . . you got it . . . "Deep in the Heart of Texas."

The Dallas Cowboys Cheerleaders' Show Group traveled the world to entertain our servicemen—Korea, Greece, Crete, Italy, Sicily, Greenland, Iceland, Portugal, Germany, the Philippines, Turkey, Lebanon, the Sinai Peninsula, and Diego Garcia, a tiny footprint in the Indian Ocean. We staged our show wherever we could—an airplane hangar in Germany, a crowded theater in Turkey, a makeshift stage on the deck of an aircraft carrier. We made an unscheduled stop at a submarine that had been at sea for 57 days, and even performed and stayed overnight in the Marine barracks in Lebanon that were to be blown apart six months later. The place Suzette and I remember most vividly, however, is Korea.

We arrived in a helicopter during a blizzard to a place that looked like Alaska—completely white. We looked out the window and couldn't see a thing, just snow whistling around the copter. We were thinking, God, are we going to make it through this? But we had to forget our fear of crashing because we were there to do a job.

It was so cold I slept, ate, and even cleaned up in my coat. The only time I took if off was to perform. I've never experienced that kind of cold. We would put the hood of the parkas together and breathe in each other's face to try and stay warm. . . . Nothing worked.

The one day we were allowed off we took a bus to the shopping district in Seoul. We ran from hut to hut in −22 degree weather, huddling around fires the merchants had built to keep warm as they worked. After buying hundreds of trinkets, I ended up back in the bus, my mittens on my feet, my entire body numb.

★

DEEP IN THE HEART OF TEXAS

The helicopters took us to isolated bases along the Demilitarized Zone separating North and South Korea. We visited six bases a day for two weeks over the Christmas holidays. Just isolated hilltops, little quarters that served as a mess and a barracks.

We would breakfast with the boys. Then, we'd go to another camp and have lunch. Then, we'd do a performance somewhere else, and then dinner in another place, and finally, another show at night—signing autographs the whole time. The only break we'd have was a half-hour once during the day. Then, we'd get up the next day and do it all over again. We'd go to bed around 2 and wake up at 5:30. Most of the time we didn't even take our makeup off. There was no time for illness or exhaustion. We'd just get up and take a quick shower and go.

The soldiers we visited were in pathetic shape emotionally. They were stationed for months at a time in little hillside camps in which there weren't even any trails except for the path worn out to the chopper pad. There was no way out of there except by helicopter. Nothing to do except sit on that hilltop and stare at the other hundred or so GIs with us.

There they were, stuck in a godforsaken spot in South Korea, halfway around the world from Dallas, and suddenly, as if their wildest fantasies had been granted, here come the Dallas Cowboys Cheerleaders. As soon as they saw us, most of them just started crying. One moment they were in hell, the next they were in the company of beautiful American girls carrying American flags, hugging and kissing everybody in sight.

It was a moving experience for those soldiers and for us. One of the Marines wrote *Joyce Stone* when she got home and said he had a dream about an explosion and a building on fire. He broke in, took her in his arms, and rescued her. They went off to an island and lived the rest of their lives

★

in happiness. That's what we meant to those guys. We were a dream of hope to them.

Many men would give us the addresses and phone numbers of their families—"Please call my mother and tell her I'm okay. . . . "Tell my wife I love her," or, "I've got a little girl at home and I've never seen her. Please give her a kiss for me."

When we got home we'd call and the wives and mothers thanked us all over again. It was wonderful.

One moment in particular has stuck with me and it haunts me to this day. It was Christmas Eve. We were being briefed by the Commanding Officer as we strapped on our flak jackets and helmets. We loaded into jeeps and headed toward Guard Post Collier and Oulette. Duty here changed every three weeks—proximity to the northern border created incredible stress.

There was a soldier named Phil who had been in Korea for almost 18 months and he was in his second tour in the DMZ, in a place where the air just about crackles from the tension. Phil took me up into the tower that faces the South Korean side. He handed me a pair of binoculars and had me look across the barren area to the towers on the Communist side. A huge wire fence with rolls of barbed wire across the top were the only thing that separated the two armies. Beyond the fence loomed a make-believe city that was supposedly constructed by the North Koreans as propaganda to lure the South Koreans over the line during the war of the 1950s. The city was only a front; no one actually lived there. It was more beautiful than any Hollywood set that I had ever seen. I was in a state of shock as Phil said, "Focus inside the tower. Look right inside."

"All right." And there in the tower was an enemy soldier staring back at me through his binoculars. It was a chilling feeling and a flash of stark reality, standing there only one

★

step away from lost freedom. I began to shake right there. Phil put his arm around my shoulder.

"For the last three or four months I was sure I was going to die here," he sobbed. "I kept having these dreams that I was in a bag in the back of a helicopter and they were flying me out of Korea. I was dead but at least I was finally going home. And then the chopper got shot down and I was going to have to stay here forever.

"I never thought I'd ever see America again, and if I did, I was sure it could never live up to my dreams. And then you girls arrived and I knew I wouldn't be disappointed. I'm certain now I'm going to make it back alive. I don't know why. I just know it now."

When I saw the Communist soldiers looking back at me, I realized how important these American soldiers were to our freedom and the tremendous sacrifices they made for us.

After Korea, the Show Group was flown on another USO tour to the Indian Ocean and Saudi Arabia. The Cheerleaders went to a naval base on the island of Diego Garcia where the humidity was stifling. They flew to Saudi Arabia where they boarded a helicopter that took them to a fleet of naval ships not far from Oman. The finale of the tour was a New Year's Eve show aboard the aircraft carrier USS *Constellation*, so large it had been dubbed "the floating city."

The helicopter that had transported the Cheerleaders was barely large enough for the group. The girls were strapped in, the engines revved up, and bang! They were out of there. When they landed on the *Constellation* it was just like in *Top Gun*.

The New Year's Eve show on the *Constellation* was unforgettable. The Cheerleaders were going to go on at 10:30 so that they'd reach the finale at the stroke of midnight. They had all day to visit and tour the ship. The guys, of course, were great hosts.

★

Several other ships had pulled up alongside of the *Constellation* and dropped anchor so they could also see the show. By the time it started, there were something like 30,000 anticipating the Dallas Cowboys Cheerleaders. Men filled every imaginable inch of the ships, spilling over five different decks, and stacked on top of the massive guns and up on the bridge. It was a magnificent sight. . . . A balmy tropical evening with the full moon hanging over the Indian Ocean. And all the sailors were decked out in their dress whites, the ship draped with banners and bunting of stars and stripes.

When 12 girls pranced onto stage wearing those famous Dallas Cowboys Cheerleaders uniforms, the men let out a roar that dwarfed anything the girls had ever heard. It rocked that mammoth ship. As they danced, the roaring and whistling grew with each number.

After two numbers, the girls exited the stage in a rush to make their next costume change in the back of the chopper. And Lisa slinked onstage, draped in a sequined red, white, and blue outfit cut in two inch strips from her waist to her knees. Each step she took revealed those beautiful legs of hers. She started singing and the roar the men let out made the deck vibrate. Then she singled men out to come onto the stage with her and she sang into their eyes and the whole ship swooned, "Oooooooooooooouuuuuuuuuhhh!"

"I love you, Lisa," someone yelled and she yelled back, "I love you too!" And the roar about blew her into the water.

After Lisa got their hearts pumping, the rest of the girls came out for their famous kickline routine, which wasn't easy because the ship would list to the left and they'd go right. But they didn't mind. On a night like that they didn't care about anything except the moment.

At 11:50, the Captain of the "Connie" came up on the stage with them and a ceremony was held to reenlist six men. It

★

DEEP IN THE HEART OF TEXAS

was minutes away from midnight and a 21-gun salute brought in the New Year.

The girls started singing "God Bless America" and everyone joined in. The Dallas Cowboys Cheerleaders, Suzanne Mitchell, the Admirals of the fleets, the Captains, the officers, and 30,000 men. Thirty thousand strong, emotion-charged male voices singing about their homeland.

"GOD BLESS AMERICA! LAND THAT I LOVE!" Booming out across that faraway ocean.

Everyone on that ship was crying. The men were coming up on stage in droves without panic or shoving. They just broke rank and climbed up on stage and everyone kissed and hugged.

The girls were standing in the center of this incredible storm of passion. They hadn't just put on a great show for an audience of fans. They had tapped into the emotions of a nation's pride. They had gotten down into the soul of these lonely men, thousands of miles from home and family, and applied a salve of love to their deepest wounds. The best, the most beautiful, the sexiest, the most wholesome All-American girl from next door had come to them in a dream and sworn her love and gratitude. And those men knew that what they were doing was right.

Everyone sang for half an hour, chorus after chorus.
"FROM THE MOUNTAINS, TO THE PRAIRIES,
"TO THE OCEANS, WHITE WITH FOAM
"GOD BLESS AMERICA! MY HOME SWEET HOME!"

The Cheerleaders had never felt that much elation and pride in their lives. They stood there embracing our boys, floating in the middle of a vast ocean, singing to the pitch black heavens about their love for a way of life in which dreams can come true.

★

19

In spite of her demanding nature, the girls had a certain respect for Suzanne. After all, it was she who had pushed them to succeed far beyond what they ever thought they could achieve. Even later, after their cheerleading days were over, they would use what they had learned from Suzanne to succeed in other careers.

Suzanne was a complicated woman who rarely let anyone get close. It was sometimes difficult to believe that she had our best interests in mind. Oftentimes our best interests conflicted with those of the Dallas Cowboys. And to Suzanne the Dallas Cowboys were always the bottom line.

To most of us Suzanne was like the pieces of a puzzle. Who she was or why she did the things she did will probably always remain a mystery to us. And I think that's the way she wanted it.

Every once in awhile however, we caught little glimpses of her that helped us put just a few of the pieces together. One of those instances occurred the week we were practicing for our Tangerine Bowl half-time performance.

The temperature hovered in the teens all that week in Dallas, but of course Suzanne had us out there in Texas Stadium everyday going through our routines. Heat or cold never made any difference to her. It was so brutal that the field crew had to shovel snow off the field, then roll the tarp back so we could practice. Ice rain came swirling through

★

the big hole in the roof of the stadium and ripped through our skimpy warm-ups and we froze.

When we performed at games, rarely were we allowed to wear anything but the uniform, no matter what the weather. During the first half of the game we had to be in the shorts and halter top. We'd walk out of the dressing room and that icy wind would come whipping down the tunnel and we'd freeze on the spot.

Everybody in the stands would have blankets, arctic jackets, portable heaters, ear muffs, fur coats. And we'd be pleading, "Suzanne, can we at least wear our warm-ups?"

"Absolutely not! The fans pay to see you in your uniforms," she'd say while bundled in a carmel-colored fox jacket. We cheered hot or cold, sick or lame.

During the first months of the season we fought a different kind of problem—dehydration. We were never allowed to drink much water. That was to prepare us for performing in the heat. Occasionally, girls would even pass out at practice. I don't know why one of us didn't die of dehydration. Temperatures often topped 120 on the field during games and while we rehearsed. It was inhumane to limit water intake in that heat and humidity. The players drank constantly but not the Cheerleaders. In fact, a lot of the girls were afraid to get a drink during a game because they knew those binoculars were on them constantly.

We were also plagued by injuries. Many of the Show Group girls suffered from chronic ailments. There were girls with ankle problems, knee problems. It was like a clinic. Lisa had arthritis in her shoulder. *Dolores* had broken bones in her foot and was given shots to keep going.

Zee walked around with ice bags on her knees all the time. And once a week she went to the doctor and had her knee drained. He'd pull out three big syringe fulls of fluid every week and then shoot her with cortisone.

★

That week of the Tangerine Bowl, Suzanne didn't show up for the first three days of practice. That was very strange because she never missed anything. The fourth night we were already out on the field freezing when she finally arrived.

None of us recognized her at first, hobbling down the steps of the stadium with a cane. She could hardly move. Her hands were drawn up into fists, her back slumped over as she walked. Her hair was pushed under a scarf and she had on a pair of gold lamé houseshoes. She sat down on the bottom step of the stands and every once in a while she'd scream something. "Laurie! Get moving!" But that was it.

Suzanne had arthritis. She lived in a lot of pain. How much pain, none of us will ever know. Once or twice a year her arthritis would flare up badly.

Suzanne never wanted us to see her in that condition. But she had missed so many practices that week, she had to show up. She never permitted us to show her any sympathy though. That would be a sign of weakness. Joy made the mistake of coming up to her during a break.

"How are you feeling, Suzanne?" she asked.

"Don't worry about me, young lady! Your job is to learn your routines!"

"Yes, maam. I just thought—

"It's not your place to think."

As cold as she was to us, however, it was hard not to feel sorry for Suzanne. And it wasn't just the physical pain for which we were sympathetic. Her life seemed so empty. She had been divorced for years by the time she became our director, and her life appeared to be devoid of anything we recognized as love. She had an old dog named "Sugar" that followed her around but that was about it. I never ever saw her out socializing or having fun at anything other than Cowboy Cheerleader functions.

★

DEEP IN THE HEART OF TEXAS

She had very little in life except the Dallas Cowboys Cheerleaders. Of course, a person who has a family could not commit herself to something as completely as Suzanne did to the squad. Every breath she took was spent thinking about the Cheerleaders.

Suzanne acted as emcee during many of our Show Group performances. During one of the costume changes, Suzanne would often come out on stage and warm up the crowd or keep the show going. She was usually dressed in some fantastic outfit: a number that barely covered anything. Sometimes it would be a red leotard sprinkled with white and blue sequins, topped off with a red cowboy hat, suntan pantyhose, and white cowboy boots or a Cowboys football jersey, pantyhose, and high heels—and nothing else.

That was the paradox. She would come to practice in an old black sweatshirt, old black jeans, and houseshoes, with her hair in a ponytail. But at shows she was dressed to the nines.

During one show we did, she wore a white fringed leotard cut very high on her hip, with a neckline that plunged down the front, white boots, and a white Cowboy hat.

"Okay," Suzanne shouted. "What if I told you I have a deck of cards with a picture of each girl on the front? All your favorites."

The crowd roared.

"I'm going to let y'all have a chance at one. How about if I throw them out to you."

Roar!

Flirting with the audience the whole time, asking a few of them to come up, putting her arm around them—she was in heaven.

"Now, who is a Dallas Cowboys football fan?"

Once again the audience exploded with hoops and hollars.

★

"How many are Dallas Cowboys Cheerleaders fans?!!" The entire place vibrated with whistles, cheers, and applause. Suzanne then began tossing handfuls of autographed Cowboy pictures.

Over the years we all heard of cases where Suzanne would take care of a girl in serious trouble, take her under her wing and protect her. If a girl was in a desperate situation, Suzanne would come to the rescue. She seemed to want to help any girl who had it hard in life or came from a real tragic background. If a girl came around with a real hardship story, Suzanne would mother her. If there was a wounded one, she'd do anything for her.

Laurie Howard was a perfect example. She had been retired as a Cheerleader for several years and had moved to Arkansas. She and her husband, Andy, had two sons, Teddy and Jack. Unfortunately, the marriage had not been a happy one. The young couple fought frequently and Laurie was concerned about the boys growing up amid the constant friction.

Laurie knew she had to get out, but she didn't know where to go. She had painted a picture-perfect homelife for all of her friends. She didn't have money for an extended stay at a hotel and she couldn't go to her mother's house. She called a friend and she had told Laurie not to stay with her mother if Laurie wanted to make a clean break of it.

She needed somewhere to go, someone to turn to. Frantically going through her address book she ran across Suzanne's name. Well, she thought, I'll call Suzanne and see if she has any idea who might help. Suzanne had always seemed to have an answer for every problem in the past. Surely she would now.

Laurie hadn't spoken to Suzanne in several years but she had a feeling Suzanne might be able to help her. Suzanne

★

knew a lot of people in Dallas and Laurie thought she might know of someone who could help, or somewhere she and her boys could go.

"Suzanne, this is Laurie Howard. I'm in need of help." She proceeded to tell her story from start to finish. Then she asked, "Do you know any place I can go that will take my kids and me in?"

"Get your things packed up and come stay with me in Dallas."

"No, no, that's nice, thanks. But that's not why I called you."

"Pack up your things and get to Dallas immediately!" she said in a commanding voice.

"Me and my two kids?"

"Yes! Do it immediately!"

So they went there to stay the weekend. And they stayed for a month.

All around Suzanne's house was her Cheerleaders memorabilia. There were 38 different jackets and hundreds of hats, insignias, and plaques. Also, models of battleships and planes that she'd been on. She had rooms of cherished mementos from all the USO tours and appearances from all over the world. It was her life.

There were also shelves and shelves of cherished books from novels to histories to the occult, rooms full of books. In the center of the dining room was a beautiful grand piano and on the floor was an expensive rug she bought in Turkey. And everywhere there were candles—on tables and sideboards and lampstands and shelves. Suzanne would go around lighting one here and there. She loved candles.

This was a single woman's house filled with delicate and precious things collected over a lifetime, and two kids had invaded it. One of Laurie's boys would pick something up and Laurie would panic and Suzanne would say, "Relax,

★

Laurie. Those are just things. It's just stuff. They're okay."

Suzanne protected Laurie and her kids in every way. She gave her money, food, and a safe place to live. Suzanne contacted a lawyer in Dallas whom she knew and an attorney in his office took the case. Laurie didn't have a penny, but proceedings were started for a divorce and custody suit.

Suzanne mothered them. Through the night, when everyone was asleep, she patrolled the house. Laurie hadn't had anyone check on her since she was a little girl. Suzanne would tiptoe in and adjust the nightlight. Or smooth a blanket. She'd do it quiet as a cat. Laurie would wake up and think, "How did that light get on?" In the morning, Suzanne would creep around quietly closing doors so as not to disturb them, and she'd have coffee and breakfast ready for them when they awoke.

One night when Laurie was lying in bed, the door slowly opened. She lay very still and pretended to be asleep, but all the while she watched Suzanne. The children were asleep. Suzanne pulled the covers over their shoulders and gave them both a soft pat. Then she turned to make sure Laurie was all right. The faint night light illuminated Suzanne's face. Laurie peeked open one eye and saw that Suzanne had the look of a sweet angel. Laurie never forgot that moment.

On another evening, just as Laurie, the two boys, and Suzanne were all sitting down to dinner, little Teddy asked Suzanne if he could say the blessing before they ate.

"Certainly, Teddy," smiled Suzanne, and all of them folded their hands and bowed their heads.

Again, it was another moment that deeply moved Laurie.

"Suzanne, I couldn't have possibly gotten through these last few years without my deep religious convictions and neither could my kids," she said.

"Well, we all have to believe in something," replied Suzanne.

★

"What do you believe in?"

"Oh Laurie, there are many spiritual models. For instance, I know the power of crystals. And I have some crystals that I consider to be very special."

Later, after the dinner dishes were cleared, Suzanne presented Laurie and each of her two children with one of her special crystals.

"These will protect you," Suzanne explained, "and bring you good luck."

Later, long after Laurie and the boys left Suzanne and began all over again in their own home, they still never forgot Suzanne's warmth and her tender care. She had seen them through a difficult period. They missed having her check on them as they slept and they missed the conversations around the dinner table. Every time they looked at their crystals, they thought of Suzanne and the security they had felt under her roof.

That was one side of Suzanne. But, like the crystals she believed in, there were many other sides and they made up a baffling mosaic of a very complicated woman.

★

20

One evening I came to practice and a bunch of the girls were out in the parking lot huddled in a big crowd around a van.

"Stephanie! Look at this!" Laurie shouted, her face as red as a sports car. She pushed a magazine toward me. It was a December 1978 issue of *Playboy*. In it were five girls appearing in a story entitled "Pro Football's Main Attractions." The five were pictured in uniforms similar to those of the Dallas Cowboys Cheerleaders but their vests were open, baring more than the usual cleavage shown at Texas Stadium. Each girl was also featured separately on an adjoining page.

"Oh, my gosh! That's *Karen Curtis*, isn't it?"

"In the flesh," Joy laughed.

Then I looked quickly around. "If Suzanne sees this, she'll kill us. You know the way she feels about the Cowgirls."

The Dallas Cowgirls were a bunch of former Cheerleaders who formed a group to capitalize on their fame as Cheerleaders. It all happened the year before, when the Cheerleaders were filming *The Dallas Cowboys Cheerleaders, Part I*, the 1978 made-for-TV movie about the Cheerleaders, authorized by the Dallas Cowboys. It turned out to be the highest-rated TV movie of the year and the second highest of all time.

The Cheerleaders didn't get paid for appearing in this film

or in its sequel, *The Dallas Cowboys Cheerleaders, Part II*, made the following year.

Of course, Cheerleaders were used to getting nothing for making the Cowboys rich. When a giant like the William Morris Agency represents you and has you in its stable, you work. The TV and movie deals, the personal appearance bookings, the commercial endorsements never stopped. For example, four or five girls including Suzette were even featured in a hat ad that ran in *Sports Illustrated*, *Time*, and *Newsweek* for months. The Cowboys made millions off these deals.

But probably the most lucrative use of the Cheerleaders was in their endorsement of products. There were Dallas Cowboys Cheerleaders posters, playing cards, calendars, dolls, frisbees, jewelry, t-shirts, decals, bubble gum, trading cards, boots, caps, jigsaw puzzles, kids' clothing and on and on. All of it with the Dallas Cowboys Cheerleaders logo and pictures of one or more of the Cheerleaders on it, autographed and merchandised all over the world.

Sears had pictures of the Cheerleaders plastered all over their stores with a line of Cheerleaders'-endorsed merchandise. Stores from here to Tallahassee sold Cheerleaders memorabilia.

The Cheerleaders themselves never got paid for any of this. Sometimes we did get paid for personal appearances and there was fifteen dollars a game which the Cowboys lavished upon us for cheering. But for almost everything else we got nothing.

During the filming of *Cheerleaders, Part I* some of the Cheerleaders became disenchanted with this practice of nonpayment. Several of the actors from Los Angeles were telling us how badly we were getting exploited, that union scale is so much for a walk-on and so much for a speaking part. Then the actors wanted to know what we got for the poster. The

★

more we told them, the more they told us what the score was.

Texas is a non-union state so Tex and Suzanne and the producers and directors of the movie *could* get us to work for free if we were dumb enough to go for it. Which we were. Plus, they *could* get away with replaying the movie a thousand times and not pay us residuals. Which they did. And they still do today.

It was a very sweet deal. What they paid Tex and Suzanne and the Cowboys organization to deliver this bunch of lambs to the slaughter is anybody's guess.

When enough girls became disenchanted about the monetary situation, Suzanne would take the opportunity to remind us, "Ladies, the money goes to the Dallas Cowboys. You are a part of the Dallas Cowboys Organization. Whatever you do is for the honor of cheering for the greatest organization in sports. There are 2,000 girls waiting to take your place. You knew what the pay was when you joined the team."

Suzanne got rid of any girl that complained. She was looking for someone who would give everything and not expect anything in return except the satisfaction of being a Dallas Cowboys Cheerleader.

In response, these girls decided to form a group called The Dallas Cowgirls. They wanted to do all the promotions and personal appearances the Cheerleaders were doing only keep the money. Also, they did functions the Cheerleaders turned down—like performing where alcohol was served.

They then attempted to market a poster imitating the famous Cheerleader poster, but with the tops of their uniforms wide open. The Dallas Cowboys Cheerleaders successfully restrained the sale of the poster. Eventually the Cowgirls closed up shop. From that time on, we always cringed if anyone called us *Cowgirls*.

★

DEEP IN THE HEART OF TEXAS

In spite of poor pay, we were compensated for our film and TV work done outside of Texas.

One day I got a call from Bobby Sue. The producer and director had just auditioned and selected 12 of us to star on a second episode—a special—of *Love Boat*. We were two of the lucky ones chosen.

"Can you believe we'll be leaving for Los Angeles Monday? I don't know how I'll have enough time to memorize my lines," said Bobby Sue.

"You can do it if you burn the midnight oil between now and Sunday," I replied.

"Oh, I heard through the grapevine that we would probably get paid."

"No."

"Yes."

"How much?"

"Union scale."

"How much is that?"

"I don't know exactly. But it's got to be more than fifteen dollars."

We received pay for our *Love Boat* episodes because we filmed in California and the unions wouldn't let us appear unless we joined SAG. We had to get paid or the producers and the Dallas Cowboys would have been sued. We each ended up with about $1,000 and residuals. We were in heaven!

When we arrived in Hollywood to film *Love Boat*, we all had stars in our eyes. When we weren't filming, we got to visit different sets on the lot like *Charlie's Angels*, and watch Jacqueline Smith and Cheryl Ladd in action. Actually it was a toss-up as to who was doing the watching. Jodie Foster, for one, made a point of visiting the *Love Boat* set when she found out we were there.

For lunch we'd go into the Universal commissary and there

★

was Alan Alda and Loretta Swit taking a break from
M*A*S*H. We all had to restrain ourselves from running
up to them screaming, "Alan, can I pleeeee-ase have your
autograph?" because we were supposed to be stars just like
them. . . . Even if last week I was just a kid from Lubbock
cruising the Sonic Burger with Billy Joe Renfro.

Most of the crew of the Love Boat was very nice to us
which made the experience very enjoyable. But, over the
years, we did have our share of problems with unfriendly
stars.

Jane Seymour played the part of a Cheerleader in *Cheerleaders, Part I* and she was anything but that placid beauty
she comes off as.

Suzanne had picked Suzette to teach Jane our dance routines. Jane wanted to be quickly shown the steps and when
Suzette tried to refine her routine a little, Jane didn't think
it was necessary. She thought she already knew how to dance
a whole lot better than any of us. It was true that she was
much better than the other actresses, but even though the
Cheerleaders were all trying to make her feel right at home,
she was convinced that this picture was the ruination of her
career. By the end of filming, she was screaming, "This part
is destroying my movie career. I should never have done
this movie. I'll crucify my agent!"

The movie was shot at "The Scotland Yard," a disco over
by Love Field. The funny thing was, they had us there at 6
A.M. and we were shooting by 6:30. And of course, we had
to be dancing like it was midnight and we'd been partying
all night.

All we wanted was some coffee! Nobody was in too great
a mood to begin with and then we had this prima donna
prancing around, acting superior to everyone around her.
Life was generally unpleasant for the two to three weeks of
filming. Miss Seymour was rather aloof and didn't have two

★

words to say to any of us lowly little cheerleaders who were ruining her career.

Whew!

Morgan Fairchild ran a close second to Jane Seymour.

Once, in Dallas, we were doing a Variety Club Telethon and Morgan came on to do her fifteen minutes. I was the emcee for that segment along with Roger Staubach. On stage with us, was a group of the Variety Club handicapped kids. When the director motioned for Morgan to join us, she paraded in wearing a tight white dress, and as she got closer and closer, I realized that I had never seen so many layers of heavily applied makeup in my life. It looked as though it would have taken a chisel to get it off.

Then she started loving and hugging the kids. She bent down and put a little girl on her knee and smooched her cheek until the poor thing was covered in fire-engine-red lipgrease. But as soon as the camera was off her, she ignored the children and clenched her teeth. She obviously had better things to do with her time.

Miss Fairchild didn't want anything to do with those kids. But when the camera came on again she started in hugging and kissing them all over. It was disgusting.

Zee had the graveyard shift on that same telethon. She came on at 1 A.M. and that's the worst time. It's Saturday night, the bars are closing, and every guy that lost out at the local meat market calls up.

They had Zee manning the phones and she kept getting obscene phone calls. She picked up the phone once and this guy wanted to know what she did with all her dirty panties.

"For five hundred dollars, I'll tell you," Zee shot back.

Just then the camera panned over to Zee on the phone and the emcee stuck the mike in her face and asked, "What does this caller want to contribute?"

Zee looked at the guy for a second and thought, Well, he

★

wants to contribute his sperm. But instead she said, "Five hundred dollars."

"Five hundred dollars! That's fabulous! What's the caller's name?"

"He hasn't told me yet."

The emcee grabbed the phone from Zee. "Caller, this is Carl Betz. What's your name? Jimmy, how are you? We want to thank you for your contribution. It's people like you that reach down and give till it hurts, that make these telethons a success."

He handed the phone back to a smiling Zee.

On the whole though, the majority of celebrities that we met and performed with were class acts. Bob Hope, Barbara Mandrell, George Burns, the Oakridge Boys, Susan Anton, Willie Nelson, Dolly Parton, Mickey Gilley, Loretta Lynn, and Crystal Gayle, just to name a few, treated us like royalty. Many even said they were in awe of us. That really blew us all away!

A lot of celebrities had their little . . . peculiarities.

We did a personal appearance once with Larry Hagman, better known as J.R. Ewing. He was a megastar in those days, but he didn't let that get in the way of being very pleasant and friendly. Of course, we had Dallas in common.

Larry was an avid nonsmoker. He had a little hand-sized, battery-operated fan that he used to blow cigarette smoke away from him. Somebody would light up and on would go that fan. Larry wouldn't say anything, he'd just get a little sly smile on his face and point the fan and blow the smoke back in the smoker's face. It was a good thing Larry was J.R. at the time because if you blew smoke in some Texan's face, he just might put his cigarette out . . . on your nose.

Hank Williams, Jr. apparently had something against bathing.

★

DEEP IN THE HEART OF TEXAS

When we were filming *Nashville Palace*, we did a number with Hank in which he was supposed to serenade us with his country hit, "Texas Women." It's a number none of us will ever forget—much as we try.

I don't think Hank had taken a bath in a month. He had a half moon of salty sweat stains under the arms of his fancy cowboy shirt, his pants were filthy, and his hair was greasier than an old motor. He also had the habit of sitting over on the side of the stage during breaks and taking his shoes off to give his feet a breather. The problem was, he wasn't wearing any socks and the stench that came wafting across the stage made a Texas meadow muffin smell like Chanel No. 5.

For the number, we had to sit on our eight-foot stars and swoon over him while he serenaded us one by one. We were swooning all right, but it wasn't because we were faint from his charms.

When we filmed *Love Boat*, we stayed at the Beverly Hills Hotel, the famous pink palace on Sunset Boulevard where so many stars lived and supped. That's where Bogie first kissed Lauren Bacall and where Garbo did much of her hiding. We walked around the grounds of that place with chill bumps.

The second night we were there, Bobby Sue came to my room breathless.

"Stephanie! I'm in love!"

"Oh, Bobby Sue, that's wonderful! Who is he?"

"Al Corley."

Bobby Sue got typecast as the country bumpkin who falls for a guy on board. One of her co-stars was Al Corley, who was about a month away from international stardom. He had just landed the part of Steven Carrington on a new show called *Dynasty*. He was going to play the son of Joan Collins.

But, at that moment, he was still a struggling actor trying to claw his way up the ladder anyway he could.

Al was an ex-football player who'd never acted before, just a country boy from Missouri who was so good-looking the producers of *Dynasty* had to take him. They told him to lose eighty pounds and he did and they gave him the part.

When they met, Al told Bobby Sue about his luck being spotted and selected for *Love Boat*. He was a star and he was being honest. Bobby Sue fell for him.

"Well, don't just sit there. Tell me what happened today?" She sat down on the bed in my hotel room.

"Oh, it was so romantic," Bobby Sue swooned. "He took me out on his motorcycle for a short drive but we came right back and spent most of our time out by the pool. I was afraid to go too far because of Suzanne's rule that we stay near the hotel.

"And he kissed you?"

Bobby Sue blushed. Then she looked at me and she got all moony. "Yes."

"How was it?"

"Just like you dream about."

"Bobby Sue!" I screamed and hugged her. She had found what we'd all dreamed about our whole lives. A rich, handsome man who swept her away.

"Tell me everything, Bobby Sue."

Al and Bobby Sue had been by the hotel pool but they may as well have been together at Paradise Cove. They had basked in the sun and in each other's company and for Bobby Sue it was all she had hoped for in romance. Al's kiss had left the proverbial stars in her eyes.

"See you tonight?" he asked.

"Okay, if I can," Bobby Sue said.

"I'll fix it. Don't worry." And he drove off.

★

Bobby Sue was floating as he drove off. She just stood there for a while, a few feet off the ground, watching him disappear around the corner. She didn't move until he was completely gone, the sound of the city drowning out the last 'vrooom of his motorcycle. Then she turned and walked slowly through the famous pink building where movie stars lounged beside the pool talking about their movies, and agents and producers threw millions around while drinking martinis. It was just like a fairy tale, like a movie.

For whatever reasons, Suzanne permitted Bobby Sue to go out with Al. She wasn't going to tell them to us, but she had her reasons. She always had her reasons. We were all shocked because Suzanne wouldn't let us date anyone if she could prevent it. Especially not on these trips.

David Cassidy was another of the stars on our episode of *Love Boat* who had a crush on one of the Cheerleaders. *Helene McClendon* was a striking brunette to whom David took a fancy.

When he asked Helene out, she told him, "I can't go out with you. Suzanne won't let me."

So he went to Suzanne. "I want to take out Helene. I'll take the whole team out on a date if that's what it takes to be around Helene. But I'd like to be alone with Helene for a while after dinner."

"Absolutely not," Suzanne told him and walked away.

Meanwhile, Bobby Sue and Al were falling deeper and deeper in love. She was intoxicated with his kisses and the whole Hollywood romance—the pink hotel, the stars in the cantina, the makeup artist and hair stylist hovering around her for two or three hours every morning. Three months before, Bobby Sue was a student at a small college. Two months before that she was in high school in a town with less people in it than this studio. Now she was starring in

★

an episode of *Love Boat* and she'd fallen in love with a potential Hollywood star.

She didn't know what was going on or what was going to happen next. And she didn't care. It was all a great big wonderful dream come true.

Al Corley's dream however, wasn't turning out exactly like he thought it would. He called Bobby Sue at the hotel one night in a panic.

"Oh, Bobby Sue, I've got to see you, babe."

"What's wrong Al?"

"Meet me in the parking lot in an hour."

"I can't. Suzanne would kill me."

"You've got to. It's life or death. Don't worry about Suzanne. I'll take care of her."

Al had no idea what he was going to be doing when he signed his contract. He thought, Oh, boy! *Dynasty*, I've made it!

That is, until he found out what his part called for. He was going to be the first prime-time homosexual. This big hunk!

"Bobby Sue," he sighed when they embraced. "They're going to make me kiss a guy on network TV."

He was nearly in tears.

"Oh, no, Sweetie," she said.

"Yes. But it's worse than that really. I'm supposed to be in love with him!"

Al put his face in his hands and shook his head. Bobby Sue held him while Al kept muttering over and over.

"My first big break and I'm cast as a homosexual."

"You'll get plenty of great roles after this, Sweetheart!"

"Nah, I'm finished. Once they put you in a role like this, that's all you get called for. I'll be doing hairdressers the rest of my life."

★

"No."

"Yes! Those old women watching those shows believe you really are the character you play. They all think Joan Collins really is a terrible bitch. You do see what I mean, don't you Bobby Sue?"

"Yes, I do Sweetheart. . . . "

Before we went to L.A. to film *Love Boat*, Suzanne had taken us all aside. "Now, many other girls have gone to Hollywood and none of them have made it. It's a tough world out there and there are going to be a lot of men coming up to you, offering you the moon. All they want is to use you. So watch out. Come to me with any offers.

"If you stay with the Cheerleaders, you'll be important. With these Hollywood people, you'll be just another body. I wish you could read all the letters I've received from girls who tried to make it out there, begging me to take them back. But once you go, that's it. You don't get another chance with the Dallas Cowboys Cheerleaders."

Suzanne was right about one thing. We were deluged with offers during our stay in Hollywood. It was like a battlefield. The offers came flying in from all directions and Suzanne would always be there trying to shoot them down. A few offers always seemed to get through.

One evening we all got together for dinner at a trendy L.A. restaurant, Carlos 'n Charlies, and two men came over to our table. They pointed right at Loni and said, "That's her! That's the girl we want."

Loni sank down in her chair. She could feel Suzanne's eyes on her.

"We want you to be in our movie."

"Excuse me?"

"We want you for one of the leads in our new movie. You're perfect. Can we talk to you alone for a few moments over here?"

★

"I'm sorry. If you want to speak to me you'll have to do it through the lady at the end of the table."

"Yeah, who's she?"

"That's our director."

"So?"

"Well, we're Dallas Cowboys Cheerleaders and if you wish to speak to us you have to speak to her first."

"This is a joke, right?"

"No. It's not."

So they went over to Suzanne and talked a while and then left. After dinner, Suzanne came up to Loni.

"You handled that very well, Loni. I don't want you to talk with those men. They offered you a part in which I don't think you should be involved."

Loni was very curious what the movie was but she didn't dare ask Suzanne. Loni was 1,300 miles from home in a strange place and Suzanne was her only guide. So she sat quietly.

The two men, however, didn't sit quietly. They found out who Loni was and phoned and left a message at the hotel desk the next morning.

"Loni, we're producers. We have a film project ready to shoot and we've been looking for a girl to play the lead and we think you're it."

"What's the movie called?"

"*Mommie Dearest.* It's the story of Joan Crawford and we're looking for someone to play the part of her daughter opposite Faye Dunaway."

"Gee, it sounds great, but I can't."

"It's worth $150,000 plus extras."

"I can't."

"In heaven's name, why not?"

"Suzanne would kill me."

There was a casting director for *Dynasty* at the set one

★

day. He liked the way Al and Bobby Sue looked together. They were both blondes, both good-looking, and they played well together. So he came up to Bobby Sue's room one morning and asked her if she would be interested in the role of Fallon.

It wasn't long after the offer had been made that Suzanne invited Bobby Sue to have lunch with her. During the meal Bobby Sue mentioned that she had been approached about several roles on other television shows.

"Bobby Sue," Suzanne explained, "I want you to know that I don't think these parts you've been approached about are in your best interest. This sort of thing happens and more than likely they aren't even serious about the offers. I'm supposed to be looking out for you. When anyone associated with *Dynasty* approaches you, I want you to turn them down. You're young. Everything looks good to you. But these people will offer you anything."

"Yes, ma'am."

"I'm here to protect you."

"Yes, ma'am."

As Suzanne drank her iced coffee she reminded Bobby Sue that all of us were under a contract with the Dallas Cowboys Cheerleaders and couldn't enter other agreements without the organization's approval.

None of us really even read the Cheerleaders contract that we signed at the first meeting after joining the team. Suzanne shoved it in front of us and we signed. Then before the first regular season game, she gave us each our Cheerleader ring which was the only piece of jewelry we were ever allowed to wear with our uniform. After that, we felt as though Suzanne and the organization owned us—body and soul.

Suzanne had in her possession a lot of valuable property in the Cheerleaders. These girls were special in a lot of ways. The cream of any crop.

★

She wasn't going to let somebody come along and drain her talent pool no matter how good the offer or what it would mean to these girls' futures. She kept telling us over and over that there were girls waiting to take our places, even though she knew better. Sure, there were some sleazy producers and agents with sleazy offers who came along. But there were also legitimate offers from established companies and Suzanne shut them down at the door before the girls even got a chance to hear an offer. Mail addressed in care of the Dallas Cowboys Cheerleaders was screened before being delivered to us.

Suzanne was a business woman who knew she had these girls tied up tight with an illusion. And if that didn't work, she had the girls tied up in a contract.

"I'm informing you now," Suzanne told Bobby Sue, "that if these people approach you, do not pursue it. I'll take care of them. Don't talk to anyone."

Bobby Sue never brought the subject up again. She trusted Suzanne.

On her way back to her room, Bobby Sue met *Dolores Kirby* in the hallway. Dolores had a beautiful bouquet of roses with her.

Dolores was a tall blonde beauty who later became a top model in Dallas. She was featured in one of the most successful ad campaigns in airline history. Her face was plastered all over billboards at DFW Airport for a couple of years.

"Where did you get the roses?"

"Oh, Bobby Sue, I'm not supposed to tell anyone. Come in my room."

"Wow! somebody must really like you. Who bought you all these flowers?"

"Promise you won't say a thing if I tell you who it is. Suzanne will kill me if she finds out."

★

"Of course, I won't tell."

"They're from Al."

"Al?"

"Yeah, Al Corley. You know, the really good-looking blonde?"

"Yes, I know him. . . . "

21

When we left Hollywood to fly back to Dallas, Lisa promised herself that she would return to California soon and pursue an acting career. Her starring role on "Love Boat" had only whetted her appetite. She knew she wanted more. Lisa had heard how Suzanne had tried to stop the other girls when they were offered acting roles. She was determined that Suzanne wouldn't wreck her chances. Lisa had trained her whole life to be an actress and she wasn't going to let anybody blow it.

John LaRoche was one of the most powerful agents in Hollywood. He later discovered and catapulted into stardom, actresses like Michelle Pfeiffer and Kim Basinger and a whole list of others. His specialty was the petite and beautiful blonde. The one with the full lips and ice blue eyes and body that burst out of a dress.

John LaRoche! He had created more actresses in the last ten years than anyone else in Hollywood. He was the agent Lisa wanted. An actress friend of hers, starring in a television series at the time, was managed by LaRoche.

"My God," Lisa reasoned, "if John would represent me, I could be a star too."

What better way to arrange a meeting than to have her friend help.

Lisa finished out the year with the Cheerleaders and turned in her uniform. Three months later she flew to Los

★

Angeles for a two-hour meeting with John LaRoche at his office.

That day, she had to wait in the reception area for several hours, but she didn't mind. He was a very busy and important man and she was lucky he even wanted to see her. If there was any chance at all that he'd want to represent her, she'd wait a month.

Sitting in the office with her was a tall, striking blonde. They talked for a long time. The girl was also trying to become an actress. A friend of a friend had set up this meeting with John LaRoche for her.

"If you get him to represent you, you've got it made in this town, you know," she told Lisa.

"I know."

"He's taken many girls to the top. I hope he can do the same for me."

"Me too."

When the secretary finally announced that Mr. LaRoche would see her, Lisa's heart began pounding. She was finally there, in the office of a real Hollywood power broker.

"Please sit down, Lisa, and make yourself comfortable," he said.

"They engaged in several minutes of light conversation before he moved closer to Lisa.

"You're a very beautiful young girl, Lisa," he said, almost in a whisper. "And I can make you a big star. You know that, don't you?"

Lisa was almost speechless.

"Yes," she managed to respond.

"You have great potential. But that doesn't mean a thing without the right people guiding you. I want you to go home to Dallas and pack up your things and come back here and move in with me. We'll go to all the parties together. I'll introduce you to all the right people. And they'll know very

★

quickly I want you to get the right parts. I control some of the biggest stars in Hollywood. If you don't get what I want you to get, they don't get the big star. That's the way it works here."

"Oh."

"We'll put you in Strasberg. It's good for the P.R. sheet. And I want you to do *Playboy*. That's for starters. Think it over and let me know your decision within the week."

As John stood up and came around from behind his desk, Lisa's mind was racing. He walked her past the tall blonde in the reception area and opened the door for her. Lisa couldn't believe her eyes. A cab was waiting to take her back to the airport. Before motioning her through the door, John tightened his grip on her arm. "Remember my offer, Lisa."

She was 18 and she had known LaRoche for two hours when he put this proposition to her. All she had to do was say yes. All she had to do was reach out and take her dream; move in with a man she didn't know, didn't love, and become his concubine. All she had to do was go against everything her father had taught her. Lisa cried all the way back to Dallas.

★

22

W hen the season ended, Bobby Sue had decided not to come back for another year. It was a lot of work and humiliation; so she told her parents and her brother and sister and the rest of her relatives and friends that she'd cheered her last game. They were all disappointed but she wanted to return to school, and her relationship with Suzanne had disintegrated.

Bobby Sue had always been a favorite of Suzanne's, ever since she'd interviewed Bobby Sue on campus. She had molded Bobby Sue into the perfect little cheerleader and Bobby Sue followed her every suggestion. She'd changed her hair and lost weight and worked very hard. Suzanne had sent her on personal appearance after personal appearance to all the little country towns in Texas. But ever since they had returned from Hollywood, Suzanne had turned cold and Bobby Sue didn't understand why.

One day while they were in her office, Suzanne asked Bobby Sue if she was re-auditioning for the squad the following year.

"I'm thinking of quitting," Bobby Sue told her.

"Oh, Bobby Sue, you can't do that. We really need you."

"Well, I've thought it over and I don't know if I can really motivate myself to do another whole year. And cheering takes all the energy I've got."

"Oh, that's the way all the girls feel after a long season. You'll feel differently after a good rest."

★

"I didn't know you wanted me back that bad."

"Are you kidding? We need you. I've got big plans for you next year. You've got to come back. You're one of the stars of the show."

Bobby Sue was dumbfounded. She'd never heard Suzanne talk to her this way since that day in college when she'd talked her into trying out for the Cheerleaders. In fact, she'd gotten nothing but the cold shoulder from Suzanne ever since returning from California.

Bobby Sue was on a cloud for four months as she worked out everyday to get in shape and put together a dynamite routine for tryouts. She had to show Suzanne that the faith she had in her had been wise. For hours she worked on the routine, and when tryouts rolled around, she was ready.

The football season was over. At one of the last practice sessions for a telethon, Texie and Zee were talking.

"Zee, I understand you're thinking of quitting."

"Yes, I have been. You know what a struggle it's been for me to keep up with the dancing. I didn't have all the formal dance training that most of the other girls had."

"Yes, I know."

"When you said, 'Up to the bar!' that first time, I thought I'd order a Jack Daniels," Zee laughed.

Texie smiled. "I know it's been rough for you, Sandy. But I'm proud of you. You've come a long way and have been a good student. Of course, you can do what you want, but I really think you should try out again next season."

When Zee left the practice session, she was encouraged.

It wasn't as if she needed to spend the next four months working her tail off preparing for another year as a Dallas Cowboys Cheerleader. But with that vote of confidence, why not?

Loni was a different case. One day she called Debbie Bond, Suzanne's new assistant, from the airport. "Debbie would

★

you please tell Suzanne I'll be a couple of minutes late. I was away on business."

"Okay, but hurry!"

"I will."

"When Loni walked into Texas Stadium, the squad was still lined up in the tunnel and she thought, "Oh, good. I made it. They haven't gone out yet."

Suzanne was standing alone at the 50 yard line when she spotted Loni.

"Loni!" yelled Suzanne. Her name echoed throughout the stadium. "Get over here!"

Loni walked out to the middle of the field.

"Didn't Debbie tell you I was going to be late?" she asked.

"I don't care. I don't want to hear it. You're fired!" Suzanne's face was red and her eyes were on fire and she was still screaming at the top of her lungs even though Loni was standing right next to her.

Of course, all the girls heard it and so did the maintenance crew in the stadium. All anyone could hear was Suzanne's shrill scream.

"I don't want to ever see you again. Just leave!" Then she stuck her face up next to Loni's and screamed, "Leave!"

Loni was devastated. She left the field crying.

Four days passed before she mustered up the courage to call Suzanne. No luck. She tried several times with no success. Finally, Loni's phone rang. On the other end was Debbie Bond.

"Loni, what's up? What's the problem?"

"What do you mean, what's the problem? Suzanne fired me!"

Loni realized she was still in shock but somehow she managed to ask Debbie when she should turn in her Cheerleader uniform.

"Loni, don't be ridiculous. Don't you think I would have

★

heard it if you were fired? Why don't you come on down. I think you and Suzanne need to talk."

Loni dutifully drove to Suzanne's office the following day. She left her uniform in its place of honor in the closet, and only brought along plenty of butterflies in her stomach.

When they were comfortably seated, Suzanne looked at her truant Cheerleader and smiled.

"Loni," Suzanne began quietly, "believe it or not, I've had my share of problems too. I do understand what you're going through. I've been through plenty of hard times myself."

Suzanne's smile and gentle words put Loni at ease. Then Suzanne began again.

"Now, let's put those bad times behind us and think about the present."

"Okay," managed Loni.

"Suppose you tell me what you were doing the other day that caused you to be late for practice," continued Suzanne without missing a beat.

"Uh . . . I was away. I was away on business."

"Business," said Suzanne, flashing her best smile, "cannot get in the way of being a Dallas Cowboys Cheerleader. There's a time and a place for business."

Loni began to squirm. Suzanne pressed on.

"And speaking of business, Loni, to what business are you referring?"

"Well, Suzanne," Loni beamed. "I design and manufacture all kinds of beautiful hair accessories."

"Loni," Suzanne said, "don't you realize you're just following a trend? Hair accessories are a fad that will pass."

Loni was devastated. In a single blow, Suzanne had thoroughly demolished the one thing that Loni still believed was her most outstanding attribute—her creative talent for design.

★

DEEP IN THE HEART OF TEXAS

Loni's heart was beating a mile a minute. But through the tears welling in her eyes, she could also see the wheels were turning twice as fast in Suzanne's mind. After what seemed an eternity, Suzanne turned back to Loni and sighed deeply. Then she spoke once more.

"You have simply got to straighten up, Loni. I mean it. We've got no room in this organization for girls whose minds are on outside business. You're a Dallas Cowboys Cheerleader! Teamwork is what it's all about. Do you understand?"

Loni was able to manage a weak "Yes ma'am." Her eyes were on the carpet.

"No! Look at me, Loni! Do you really understand?"

Suzanne was out of her chair, and in front of the dejected Cheerleader.

"You're not Loni Wallace. You are a Dallas Cowboys Cheerleader. You can't act or think any way you choose. You must understand that. You represent all of Texas. All of America."

Suzanne returned to her chair behind the desk.

"Loni, I'll tell you what. Tex Schramm gave me a chance and now I'm going to give one to you. I'll see you tonight at practice. Seven o'clock sharp!"

Loni left Suzanne's office in a haze. She felt confused. She knew she had overstepped the boundaries once again. And had gotten by with it. But now Loni believed her self respect was gone and she felt empty inside. She felt like she had not only let down Suzanne but her sister Cheerleaders as well. Loni wasn't sure if she had any self worth left.

"But at least," Loni said to herself as she slid behind the wheel of her car, "I'm still a Cheerleader—a Dallas Cowboys Cheerleader. They haven't taken that away from me. Not yet."

* * *

★

Ironically, one of the tryout finals was held on Mother's Day. *Trudi Ragsdale* and Bobby Sue presented a bouquet of flowers to Suzanne.

"Thank you Suzanne for being like a mother to us all," Trudi said, and the rest of the team cheered.

When the names of the girls who'd made the team were announced, Bobby Sue and Zee and Trudi were out. Loni was still in. Hers was the last name called. She was in. But she didn't feel she deserved to be.

The four girls sat there in stunned silence. Everybody was yelling. And the four of them just sat there looking at the celebration going on around them. None of them could believe it. Zee couldn't get out of her chair. Bobby Sue thought there was a mistake. She couldn't believe it because nobody had ever done anything like that to her before. She wasn't raised that way.

When Trudi didn't make it back, she fell apart right there. Fell apart and put her face in her hands and started crying.

"I played by the rules. My dancing was good. I wasn't into drugs. I didn't date the players. I loved being a Cheerleader," Trudi sobbed. "What did I do wrong? Why? Why? I played by the rules."

She collapsed on the ground. "I'll do anything. I've got to be on the team," she wailed.

Zee was angry. On the one hand she thought to herself, "Be nice, Sandy." But part of her wanted to tell the judges off. "Hey, Dallas Cowboys Cheerleaders are no longer a part of our life anymore," Zee thought. "We just got kicked off the squad. It doesn't matter anymore. Let's not waste our energy."

Suzanne sat in her judging chair, emotionless behind her dark sunglasses.

Zee went over and put her arm around Trudi and hugged her.

★

"Don't give the judges the satisfaction of thinking this team is the most important thing in your life," Zee told her, "because it isn't, Trudi." And she helped Trudi to her feet.

"Listen, everybody else wanted you on the team. These are just a few people who don't want you. Take your misery with you. Don't let them see how you hurt because they are not going to change their minds."

As they left, Zee's mind was racing. Why did we have to go through this humiliation?"

"I loved being a Cheerleader. But I could never understand why they had to play mind games."

★

23

While Kim, Lisa, and Cooki were using coke to get high and party, or dance, Loni was using it more for emotional stability. When Loni felt down in the dumps, that life was slowing down or when she could see maybe it had gotten out of control, she'd snort to keep going. Loni knew there was something behind her, something she feared, and it was gaining on her. She could feel its foul breath behind her and she'd snort and zoom off and leave the beast in the dust for a while. She had the fuel she needed to put miles between her and the beast. All she hoped was that the engine would hold out. She just wanted to get a little bit farther ahead so she could pull off somewhere and get a rest. Just a little rest. But as soon as she did, when the motor slowed down from its insane revving, she could feel the beast, she could hear it coming to devour her.

Loni was underweight, overworked, hysterical, strung out and ready to explode. And she was about to get dropped off a very high cliff.

Johnny's friend, Eddie, came over a couple of nights after tryouts. Johnny had been gone for six weeks and hadn't called or written or even told Loni where he'd gone. He just left her in the house with a kilo of coke.

She was sitting on the kitchen table crying when Eddie came in. "Loni what's the matter?" And he took her in his arms and held her and she cried some more.

★

"I need Johnny to be here now and he's gone."

"Loni, you know Johnny's not coming back."

"What do you mean?"

I can't let you hang around here eating yourself up over Johnny, because he's not coming back."

Loni knew Eddie was right. Johnny had been gone more and more lately on trips. And she knew he was seeing other women around Dallas, especially when she was away on personal appearances.

"He's got a girlfriend in Mexico. That's why he's gone all the time."

Loni was crying softly while Eddie laid out the whole truth for her. "He's just waiting for you to get the hint and leave." He rested his hand on her shoulder while she cried.

"Look Loni, it's your birthday tomorrow night, right?"

"How did you know?"

"When a guy's in love with a girl, he always knows her birthday."

"What do you mean by that?"

"Do I have to say it any plainer?"

"Yes, I think you'd better."

"I'm in love with you Loni. I've been in love with you ever since Johnny brought you home."

"But you've been a good friend to me."

"Sure and to Johnny too. But I began to hate him because of the way he's treated you."

Loni looked at Eddie. She had always liked him a lot. He was funny and very good-looking. Much better looking than Johnny. He was wild like Johnny, too, but all of Johnny's friends were wild, living in the fast lane of a very fast city.

"Come on, Loni. Let's go celebrate your birthday. Why sit around her and get all morose? Let's snort some coke and hit it. Come on! We'll eat at the Mansion. Then we'll go

★

dancing at every dive in town. Let's burn the town down. You don't turn twenty every day you know."

So they did.

Eddie was a snappy dresser, and he liked to dance—a toreador in the ring of love. That night, they whirled around the dance floor for hours, going from Elan's to Cafe Dallas to Humperdink's. They had a ball, laughing and dancing and drinking and snorting and they ended up sleeping together at Eddie's place.

When they got up in the morning, they drove over to Johnny's, packed up Loni's things and ran away to Florida to live together. Loni wanted a new life. She didn't want to be a Cheerleader anymore or be reminded of it every day. She didn't want to be in love with Johnny. She didn't want to see Suzanne. She just wanted out of the whole mess. And Eddie was going to rescue her.

He was a bit slick for a knight and his trusty steed was mechanical, but here was a man who had promised to take her away from this nightmare and love her until they died.

Eddie had a kilo of cocaine with him in the van and that lasted a few weeks. They had fun driving down to Florida. They stopped in New Orleans for four days and ate until they nearly exploded. It was the most food she'd eaten in a year and she was feeling better already.

Eddie had promised her that when the kilo was gone they'd stop doing cocaine, get cleaned out, and try to get healthy— just lie in the sun and start feeling right again. And Loni couldn't wait to see the last of it, the last of that life that had turned into a monster in Dallas.

When they got to Florida though, the merry-go-round continued. Eddie started to act strange. Loni wanted to get a little place by the beach, something not too expensive so they could live comfortably for a year and not worry about

★

money. But Eddie insisted on renting a twentieth floor penthouse condo on the beach in a building with heavy security.

"I want to be able to see what's coming at me," he said to Loni as he stood on the balcony of the condo.

The way the condo was situated, backed against a jetty on a private beach, the only access to the beach was through the security guards downstairs or by boat from the ocean.

Loni went along with Eddie. It was his money. He was taking care of her, paying for everything. If he wanted to spend all that money on this place, that was all right with her. It was a beautiful apartment in a beautiful spot. They'd make love every night out on the balcony as the sun went down and then go out to dinner.

About three weeks after they'd snorted the last of the cocaine, Eddie came into the bedroom.

"Boy, I really feel like a little of the old Vitamin C tonight, don't you?"

"I guess, but I thought we were all out?"

"Oh, we are but I think I know where I can get some more. How about it? We'll get high. See a movie."

"If you want."

This went on for a couple of weeks. Whenever Eddie felt like snorting, he'd "go out" for some more. Finally, Loni confronted him.

"Where are you getting the coke?"

"You know the storage units downstairs?"

"Yeah."

"It's in there."

"How much is there?"

"Ten keys."

"My God, where did you get it?"

"I got it, okay."

"No, it not okay. Where did you get it?"

"I stole it from Johnny."

★

"Oh, my God. That means they'll be looking for us. Do you know what this means? Do you know what this means!"

"What does it mean?"

"It means we're dead. You didn't steal that from Johnny. You stole it from a bunch of hard cases. And they're not going to stop looking until they find us."

Eddie looked at her for a long time and then took a long, slow drink of his beer.

"Johnny won't tell them, if he knows you're with me."

★

uzette and I both retired from the squad after the 1981–82 season. Three years later, in 1985, my younger sister, Sheri, made Cheerleader and continued the tradition of the Scholz sisters as Dallas Cowboys Cheerleaders. But the tradition and the dream ended abruptly when Sheri quit the team two games before the end of the season. It wasn't too long after Sheri's resignation that Mother and Daddy went their separate ways.

All of this happened right in the middle of the Bust, when the Texas economy died overnight from a massive dose of greed. The foundation of the Dallas boom had been built on a fragile base of easy money, spiralling real estate prices, and plain old fraud. When the Arabs opened the oil spigots and glutted the market, the price of Texas crude took a nosedive of monumental proportions.

The Bust was particularly devastating because of its swiftness. A collapse with no time to bail out. The price of oil was thirty-four dollars a barrel one day and a month later it was twenty, then fifteen, finally bottoming out at ten dollars a barrel; which meant that if you had borrowed money to drill a well on the assumption that oil prices would be thirty dollars a barrel you had no chance of repaying the loan.

The Bust took on a life of its own, gaining frightening momentum. It was a tidal wave of bad debt that drowned nearly every high roller in Texas in a sea of red ink. Over-

★

night, men who were living like potentates one minute, were unable to make a payment on their car the next minute. In fact, they couldn't make any payments.

When the Bust came, everyone started calling in notes all at once. This guy wanted his money from that guy, and that guy wanted his money from the next guy to pay some other guy who was in hock up to his Stetson. And on and on and on and on, until the whole house of cards collapsed. Nobody was getting paid because nobody had any money to make any payments.

If the Boom had continued in Texas, there wouldn't have been an S & L scandal, at least not right away. The acceleration of prices, the tremendous fat created by the Boom, might have let the party go on for another decade. But when the collapse of oil prices came, the truth about land flips and loan flops concocted by the S & L con men was exposed.

Lots of folks had been in on the scam. Tax shelters were a popular investment in those days. And many people leveraged themselves to the hilt in order to invest. That was the smart way to do it. Use other people's money. Put up $100,000 to buy a piece of property that would give back a $250,000 tax break. Investors were making money! They didn't care what happened to the property or to its value. It was the tax shelter that was making the money. The intrinsic value of the property to the community was never considered. Let it go to pot! In this kind of deal the property was worthless, the scam was everything.

"Rolling stock" was another shelter. The government gave a tax break to the owner of a railroad car as a stimulus to business. Investors who bought these rolling machines could lease them to a company and the company wouldn't have to invest money to buy railroad cars. The lease would pay the investor's note on the boxcar and he'd depreciate the car for his tax break.

★

DEEP IN THE HEART OF TEXAS

It was the sweetest deal in the world! The only problem was that everybody wanted in on the deal and in no time there was a glut of railroad cars. The price to lease a car fell like a rock. In the end, some dentist in Irving got stuck with eight railroad cars he didn't know what to do with. He was drilling teeth all day long to support a bunch of box cars collecting dust. But he still had to keep up the payments on the note that came due every month. So he'd try to unload the boxcar and end up losing all of his investment on the deal.

The swan dive of oil prices put a stress on the Texas economy that it couldn't withstand. The economy was built on a base of fake credit, fake accounts, fake deals put together by phonies—fake social events filled with fake people. The whole thing was fake. Just like everyone knew deep in their hearts.

The Texas economy turned out to be all smoke and mirrors. And when the smoke blew away and the mirrors shattered, when we could see all those sleight-of-hand land swaps and silver straddles and rolling tax shelters for what they were, it was too late.

Texans were in a state of shock. A credit-drunk society, dizzy from conspicuous extravagance, was reduced overnight to a cash-poor community scrambling to make ends meet. The Texas economy was dealt a knockout punch so swift and devastating, it left Texans in a financial and spiritual stupor. Everything around them was collapsing. Their vaunted recession-proof economy was shattered. Their heroes were crooks. Was there nothing of substance there all along? Was there nothing of real value left? How deep did Texas's loss of trust go?

During this tragedy, the Dallas Cowboys were at center stage. Team owner Clint Murchison's family wealth, like all fortunes in the Lone Star State, was tied to black gold.

★

Mounting claims on overdue debts, the majority of which were real estate deals gone sour, put Murchison's back to the wall. He felt like one of the defenders of the Alamo. Murchison watched his net worth of millions shrink until he found himself in bankruptcy court. Finally, in 1984 it got so bad that he had to sell his beloved football team.

Murchison had purchased the franchise back in 1960 for a mere $600,000—a respectable sum back then, but only "walking-around change" for the Texas titans in the eighties before their oil bubble burst. After 24 glorious years of owning "America's Team," Murchison peddled the Dallas Cowboys to an eleven-member limited partnership headed by fellow Texas tycoon, Bum Bright. The asking price was $65 million for the team and an additional $25 million to cover the stadium lease. Bright and his partners were able to shave $10 million off the total and wound up shelling out a cool $80 million, reportedly the largest amount ever paid for a professional sports team.

Bum Bright, the new majority owner of the proud Cowboys, left a corporate job with Sun Oil in the late sixties to become a successful wildcatter. He amassed a diversified fortune from oil and gas, banking, trucking, and professional sports. Unfortunately his interest in the Savings and Loan industry did not fare as well as his other endeavors. With more than 1 million shares, Bright was the largest stock holder in Republic Bank Corp. He engineered the merger with InterFirst Corp. to form First Republic Bank which, hurt by bad real estate loans and the plummeting price of oil, nearly collapsed before federal regulators bailed it out in the spring of 1988.

It was after his own Bright Banc Savings Association, once the Number 2 thrift in Texas, was taken over by the FDIC in February, 1989, swallowing up $200 million, that Bright sold the Dallas Cowboys to an Arkansas businessman named

★

DEEP IN THE HEART OF TEXAS

Jerry Jones. Jones bought the franchise for $140 million, once again a record amount which, this time, included ownership of the Cowboys' Valley Ranch complex, a state-of-the-art training facility 15 miles west of Dallas. Jones's first order of business was to get rid of a Texas icon, Tom Landry, as head coach and replace him with Jimmy Johnson, a college coach from Miami who was a long-time friend.

With the sacking of Landry, the humiliation and collapse of Dallas was complete. Even Texas's football team had turned on them. While Texans were squirming in pain from the devastation of their economy, the Dallas Cowboys, their pride and joy, gave them a vicious kick. From the proudest NFL franchise in history with twenty straight winning seasons, five Super Bowl victories, and two World Championships to a team that set an NFL record of 14 straight home losses and couldn't bribe their way into the playoffs.

The Dallas Cowboys Cheerleaders were in decline as well. In 1982, Texie Waterman called it quits. With her went the genius behind the phenomenon. And it showed immediately.

The organization replaced Texie with Shannon Baker, a former Cheerleader. Shannon was trained in classical ballet, and she took the Cheerleaders in a new direction. Suddenly, the Cheerleaders were doing small precise movements that made no sense on the enormous stage of a football field. Overnight they lost their power and pizazz. The dances were lifeless and studied instead of brash and flashy.

By the time Sheri joined the team in 1985, the golden era of America's Team and America's Sweethearts had passed.

Sheri has always been the doll of our family. She won the first Miss Teen Texas U.S.A. pageant and was runner-up for Miss Teen U.S.A., an event televised across the nation. Her face is perfect. She is also the mellow one in the family. While Suzette and I run around frenetically overachieving like mad, Sheri just kind of shows up and wins.

★

At pageants she drove Mother batty. Sheri would walk around with her shoulders hunched, looking half asleep and Mother would be frantically whispering, "Stop slouching!" But then it would be Sheri's turn to go on stage and the master of ceremonies would say, "And now we have Sheri Scholz doing her rendition of 'Don't Take Your Love Away.' " And she'd walk to the edge of the curtain and snap! She'd be on! The thousand-watt smile beamed and she'd be dancing like a dervish—all energy and glamour. There wasn't a soul in that audience that didn't fall in love with her.

Afterwards, Sheri would walk off stage and instantly revert into our laid-back sister who couldn't wait to get into a pair of blue jeans and tennis shoes.

Poor Sheri had all of us on her constantly—Mamie and Mother and Suzette and I, all type A personalities in overdrive. We all wanted Sheri to be perfect. And she was. She could sing, she could dance, and she was the most beautiful of the bunch. The problem with Sheri was that she was content to be an Indian in a family of Chiefs.

When Sheri first made the squad she was in awe of Suzanne. She thought she was a goddess and couldn't wait to meet the squad director. After the first meeting Suzanne called Sheri over.

"Miss Scholz."

She was very excited because Suzanne had singled her out. "Yes, ma'am."

"Drop five." That's all Suzanne said.

Sheri was five-foot-five and weighed 109 pounds and wore a size four.

Things disintegrated very quickly after that. Sheri for some reason could never please Suzanne. She was good enough for Miss Teen Texas U.S.A. but she wasn't good enough for Suzanne and ended up as an "alternate," a little wrinkle Suzanne had added to bring more pressure to bear

★

on the girls. During games Sheri and three other girls had to sit in the locker room under the stadium while the rest of the squad cheered.

It didn't make any difference if there were 32 or 36 girls on the field. Why put someone down in the dressing room to look at four walls? It didn't make sense. In fact, during some quarters Suzanne put all the girls out on the field and things went very smoothly.

It was the most humiliating thing to sit there in a cold, dark concrete locker room without windows and wait for Suzanne to slowly walk up the ramp and say, "You. Out! Now!"

Sheri would pray each quarter that she would get to go out. Sometimes she'd go out for a quarter or two and then she'd be pulled back in. Sometimes Sheri never went out.

One week McLean Stevenson was doing a taping with the team for the TV show *America*. They filmed a game, and of course, Sheri was sitting in the locker room during the filming. Later, when McLean walked into the locker room, Sheri felt embarrassed over his surprise at seeing four Cheerleaders in full uniform sitting on the bench in this cold little dungeon.

"What are you doing here?"

"Well, we were not chosen to go down on the field."

He got a disgusted look on his face and sat down next to Sheri.

"You had on turquoise leotards at rehearsal last night, right?"

"Yes."

"You're a great dancer. You are so pretty and so talented. What are you doing sitting in here?" He shook his head. "I don't know this organization but I don't like what I see."

The whole bubble finally burst for Sheri after a very curious incident. She had been on the team eight months and

★

in that time Suzanne had never given her one compliment. . . . Never, everything was negative. But one day Suzanne pulled her aside and said, "You're doing so good today, Sheri."

Sheri was on a cloud all day from that little insignificant pat on the back and danced every step full out. She felt elated, daydreaming all day of Suzanne's words. She could hear them in her ear being whispered over and over and over. . . . "You are doing so good today, Sheri."

Just the way she said her name, "Sheri." It never sounded so beautiful. It felt like a warm hand moving gently down the bare skin of her back. She thought, "Sheri, what a beautiful name that is. I'm so glad my mother named me that."

Sheri realized she loved Suzanne and wanted to be loved in return. It wasn't a physical attraction. Sheri wanted Suzanne to love her as a parent or teacher might. . . . to approve of her, tell her she was good, that she loved her. Sheri wanted to dance her heart out for Suzanne.

Suddenly, as she was dancing away, Sheri realized what had happened to her. She was having these feelings for a woman who had never shown her any warmth before. And at that moment it all fell apart for her, the whole thing. She looked around at the other girls and felt a deep, deep sorrow for them. Most had been led to a place that was psychologically devastating to them. They were dancing their hearts out for something and someone and they really had no idea what it was all about. They thought it was for the honor and glory of Texas, America, mother, father, friends and everything good. But maybe it wasn't.

Sheri had put all the pieces together in her mind and it wasn't a puzzle anymore. She had figured it out. It wasn't worth it.

Suzanne had crucified Sheri. She was our sister and after a while even we knew she'd had enough abuse.

★

Finally Suzette said, "Honey, you don't have to do this anymore. You don't have to make those midnight calls in hysterics to us ever again."

So Sheri called and talked to Suzanne.

"Suzanne, I want you to know I'm not coming to practice tonight and I'll be turning in my uniform."

So the next day she brought her uniform to Suzanne.

"Why did you quit?" Suzanne wanted to know.

"You drove me over the edge. I would ask you why and you would never give me an answer. I tried. I tried with all my heart to please you and it was never good enough."

"Well, Sheri,—

"Suzanne, I don't care what you think anymore. I've made my decision. I'll go on with my life. But I'm worried about the other girls. Do you know what it feels like to sit in a room all alone while the rest of the girls are out dancing on the field? It's humiliating. What you're doing to those girls is wrong. I'm gone now so it doesn't affect me anymore. But please have some feeling for the other girls."

Shortly after Sheri's resignation, Mother and Daddy divorced. Mother found the biggest, meanest son-of-a-bitch that ever breathed to represent her.

My mother's goal had always been to be the perfect wife and the perfect mother. That's how she was going to get what she wanted out of life.

Mother believed in being a Southern Lady and there was no room for the slightest deviation from that belief. She had to always be dressed perfectly, hair done, makeup done, never a chip on her nails or she wouldn't leave the house.

My mother was up at 6 A.M. everyday. She had on a beautiful silk robe, and breakfast was waiting for my father and us when we woke up.

Mother would get dressed up to take us to school, to car-

★

pool us to dancing, and to do the housework. Every night be-fore Daddy came home, she would take off all her makeup and reapply it and re-dress. And the Jungle Gardenia perfume would once again fill the air. We were always so proud of her.

Unfortunately however, no matter how often a woman goes to the beauty parlor, how many trips to Neiman's she makes, or how many facial treatments she gets, beauty fades. If her entire self-worth is based on her beauty and beauty is how she gets and keeps her man, on the horizon of every woman is a tragedy looming, growing nearer and more deadly, more inevitable with every passing day. She sees it there in the mirror staring back at her. The end of her marriage . . . the end of her dream, disintegrating as her youth disappears.

She fights the forces pressing in on her—the madness of sudden money, a society of collapsing values where the thrill of romance is mistaken for love, and where the grace and poise acquired through the years is looked upon as baggage easily disposed of.

What is there of value to sustain a marriage?

We were all at the Miss Texas U.S.A. pageant when it appeared imminent that Mother and Daddy would part. The three of us were not really surprised when the divorce hap-pened.

When Sheri left for Dallas to join the Cowboys Cheer-leaders, the marriage came quickly apart. The three daugh-ters had been the last thing holding it together. The whole family had revolved around the kids, and when Sheri left, my mother and father were left alone in the house.

My mother adjusted to our leaving and looked forward to pampering my father and to growing old together with him. My father, on the other hand, found excuses to not go home and he tried to do everything possible to defy the aging process. Divorce was inevitable. There was too much water

★

under the bridge. Mother's dream of the traditional marriage and family—the same one we all believed in—had just gone up in flames.

Our family was always looked up to in Lubbock —all the traditions of Texas and the South rolled into one gleaming package. When it fell apart, the marriage of the beautiful woman and the handsome, successful man, we all sat back— the family and the whole town of Lubbock—and asked, "What happened? Why did it all go wrong?"

★

25

There's a bumper sticker that I saw around Dallas a lot after the Bust. "Lord, please give us one more Boom," it read. "We promise we won't blow it this time."

That's the spirit of Texas. Nothing can keep us down. We just keep coming back. The "never say die" attitude is bred into Texans. It's preached to us from birth.

My mother would take us to a pageant and we might not win a trophy. But it didn't matter. We just went right on to the next challenge.

You can't keep a Texan down. The economy is already on the rebound, oil prices are up, land values are on the rise. It's a whole new day.

The Dallas Cowboys have a new coach and he's a good one. Jimmy Johnson was chosen "Coach of the Year" after the team came from the worst record in the NFL in 1989 to a 7-9 record and one win away from making the play-offs in 1990.

When Jerry Jones bought the team in 1989, Dallas fans were appalled by changes he made in the organization and shocked by his P.R. blunders. But we've rebounded. Now we're cheering as he rebuilds our sacred treasure—the Dallas Cowboys.

The Dallas Cowboys Cheerleaders are back on top, thanks

★

to Shannon Baker's new and upbeat nineties flash. She has responded to the times by teaching the Cheerleaders a wide variety of exciting and exhilarating choreographed routines. Suzette, Sheri, and I are honored to say that we were once a Dallas Cowboys Cheerleader, and we're filled with pride when we watch them perform their intricate, show-stopping numbers. They're femininity, class, and charm—still Number One in the sports entertainment world.

Ironically, it's the things people like to make fun of about Texans that are our strength. The bigness, the brashness, the extravagance. Right, we've still got the guy with the big Caddy and the diamond-studded boots wheeling and dealing like J.R. Yes, a Mercedes 560 SL is still known as a "Texas Taxi." We all still shop at Neiman's and The Cattle Baron's Ball is still packing them in.

Texans are still proud of being Texans. That will never change. Even at the nadir of the Bust, when the nation was blaming Texas for the collapse of the S & L industry, when our oil was worthless and whole shopping centers were being boarded up, Texans were still bragging about being from Texas.

Who can blame us?

Go anywhere in the world and the people there still see Texas as the heart of America. A pair of ornately tooled cowboy boots from "Big D" itself is the big prize for a cockney bloke, or a Tokyo chip salesman. To someone from Europe or Asia those boots are the real thing, a piece of American artwork, the crystallization of our national spirit. The whole world wanted to know who shot J.R., not just America. "Dallas" was watched religiously all over the world because it was about Texas and the idea of what Texans are like.

The Texas mystique is still alive and well everywhere you go. Last summer, my husband Hunt and I went to an In-

★

ternational Plastic Surgery meeting in the French Riviera and we saw Dallas Cowboys stickers and jerseys and caps just about everywhere we went. People would come up to us and ask us if we were from Texas. And then they would tell us what they thought Texas was all about.

Our entire family is doing well too. Mother and Daddy both remarried. Mother now divides her time between a penthouse in Dallas and a luxurious home in Santa Fe. Daddy's the only one left in Lubbock from our family, but he still has the Lear jet to get out whenever he needs to.

Mamie sold her home in Lubbock and now lives right down the road from her three granddaughters. She still keeps us laughing.

Suzette and Sheri and I all stayed in Dallas after our Cheerleading days were through. We all married surgeons like our father. Suzette's husband, Butch, is a general surgeon at Baylor Hospital. Sheri's husband, Bill, is about to start his residency in plastic surgery in Tennessee. My husband, Hunt, is a plastic and reconstructive surgeon in private practice here in Dallas.

Suzette is very active in Dallas charities. She's a member of the Junior League, and chaired the 1991 Yellow Rose Gala for the Multiple Sclerosis Society.

Suzette had a successful career as a nurse and office manager for Butch, and judged the Miss Texas U.S.A., Hawaii U.S.A. and Mississippi U.S.A. contests. She's choreographed hundreds of dance routines for drill teams and cheerleader squads across Texas.

She's also the only female coach of the Lake Highland soccer and t-ball teams and has taught vacation bible school and Sunday School.

Sheri did national TV commercials for Vidal Sassoon, Maybelline, and K-Mart. She was also a game show hostess and

★

a featured actress on *Dallas* and was the emcee with Bob Eubanks on the Miss Texas U.S.A. pageant.

With that perfect face, she was chosen for a clinical study that was used as an index for determining ideal facial characteristics for facial reconstruction.

After Cheerleading, I worked for Sarah Norton as a model and actress in hundreds of print ads, commercials, cable shows, and films during my five years with the agency.

We all gave up our careers to have children. Suzette has two boys—Dustin 7, and Chase 6. Sheri's little one-year-old girl is named Catherine after Mamie. And I have three daughters—Tiffany 4, Noelle 2, and my new daughter, Capri, conceived in the South of France and born in the Spring of 1991, during the rebirth of Texas.

I find myself bringing my three babies up just like my mother brought the three of us up. They're dressed in ribbons and lace with lots of pink and, of course, everything matches. Tiffany is taking tap and ballet classes and she just won the State Championship for ice skating in her division. She also got to skate with Katarina Witt during her *Vogue* layout, photographed at The Galleria where Tiffany takes her lessons. Noelle and Capri will be following in their big sister's footsteps soon. And Tiffany says that when she grows up, she wants to be a Dallas Cowboys Cheerleader just like her mommie and her aunts.

That's all right with me. If that's what she wants.

I look back on my whole experience as a Dallas Cowboys Cheerleader and ask myself, "Would I do it all again?" And I always answer what nearly every other former Cheerleader answers, "Yes, I would!"

I can't help what stirs in my soul, what makes my heart race and how my mind associates what's good and what's bad with the resounding voice of what my mother and father and grandmother taught me. What I learned as a little girl

★

growing up in Texas, growing up in America. A girl from any other country might look in utter amazement at what I put myself through.

But she's not a Texan. She's not an American. She's got her own set of illusions and myths and I've got mine, given to me almost the day I was born. With them, I try the best I can to take care of my husband and my family, and to turn my American Dreams into reality, Texas style.

★

Epilogue

Bobby Sue Peck was a model in Dallas for a while, married a rich man's son in Oklahoma, and was divorced within months. She then met and married one of the wealthiest men in America.

Sandy (Zee) was a flight attendant for a Middle Eastern airlines and a private charter airline where she and Trudi Ragsdale served as Michael Jackson's personal flight attendants on his "Victory Tour." Sandy has given up flying and has her own business as a designer of women's fashion and is happily married to the man of her dreams. Trudi was also the private flight attendant for Frank Sinatra for two years and has served the likes of Mel Gibson, Goldie Hawn, Harrison Ford, and Sylvester Stallone.

Careene Miller is a flight attendant for one of the busy regional airlines and so are Kim and Dolores Kirby and several other former Cheerleaders. In fact, the airline has been dubbed "Cheerleaders Grad School."

Lisa received a settlement from the bank for her father's death in the plane crash. She has moved to Hollywood and is pursuing a successful acting career. So far, she has had several parts on TV series and "movies of the week."

*　　*　　*

★

Loni Wallace took a long, winding road after she left Dallas. She lived in Florida for many years where she got involved with one loser after another. She got deeper into drugs and trouble and finally attempted suicide and failed. But Loni's coming back too. Since we started the writing of this book, she has been able to renew her friendships with many of her teammates and has been getting her life together. She is now working on a cruise ship, one of the "Love Boats," in fact, using her Cheerleaders charisma to ensure that the passengers are entertained.

★

Author's Note

This book was developed without the authorization of the Dallas Cowboys Football Club, Ltd., or the Dallas Cowboys Cheerleaders Organization. Neither organization has any affiliation with this book, nor are they responsible for the contents.

This is the story of life as a Dallas Cowboys Cheerleader from the perspective of former cheerleaders. Pseudonyms have been used, and identifying personal characteristics of some people depicted in the book have been changed, to protect their privacy. Each pseudonym appears in italics the first time it is used. Some of the characters are composites of representative types of persons whom the authors encountered during their years as Dallas Cowboys Cheerleaders. The pseudonyms used for those characters also appear in italics the first time they are used.

The authors have, in a few instances, combined separate incidents into single events for dramatic purposes and to protect the privacy of certain individuals.

Dialogue throughout the book has been reconstructed based on recollections of one or more of the participants.

★